LeBRON JAMES
King of Shots

by Anne E. Hill

TFCB

Twenty-First Century Books · Minneapolis

To my own sports stars, Caleb and Abby. May your dreams take you far but never so far that I can't be there to see you shine.

In loving memory of Rada Fulper Shows (1941–2009), missed each and every day. You were a dream mom in every way.

Twenty-First Century Books
A division of Lerner Publishing Group, Inc.
241 First Avenue North
Minneapolis, MN 55401 USA

For reading levels and more information, look up this title at www.lernerbooks.com.

Library of Congress Cataloging-in-Publication Data

Hill, Anne E., 1974–
    Lebron James : king of shots / by Anne Hill.
      p. cm. — (USA Today lifeline biographies)
    Includes bibliographical references and index.
    ISBN 978-0-7613-8641-4 (lib. bdg. : alk. paper)
    ISBN 978-1-4677-0154-9 (eBook)
    1. James, LeBron—Juvenile literature. 2. Basketball players—United States—Biography—Juvenile literature. 3. African American basketball players—Biography—Juvenile literature. I. Title.
GV884.J36H55 2013
796.323092—dc23 [B]   2011051270

Manufactured in the United States of America
2 – PC – 3/1/14

Lifeline BIOGRAPHIES

INTRODUCTION

The Big Moment: LeBron announces his plans for the future on live television on July 8, 2010.

"The Decision"

Cleveland Cavaliers fans were on the edges of their seats. But they weren't watching a basketball game on July 8, 2010. Instead, they were waiting to find out where National Basketball Association (NBA) superstar LeBron James was going to play in the 2010–2011 season. Twenty-five-year-old LeBron was not only Cleveland's best player. He was one of the best in the NBA. Named Rookie of the Year after the 2003–2004 season, LeBron had helped transform the Cavaliers from one of the worst teams in the league to one of the best. But his contract with the team was at an end, and he was a free agent. LeBron could join any team offering him a contract, and many teams wanted to add LeBron to their rosters.

LeBron and his management team had decided to broadcast his choice during a live television special on ESPN called "The Decision." The 6-foot-8-inch (2.07 meters), 250–pound (113.4 kilograms) forward was widely criticized for creating hype and drama by televising his announcement. But what many did not realize at the time was that the show was being broadcast from the Boys & Girls Club of America in Greenwich, Connecticut, with all proceeds going to the club to support their youth programs. More than $3 million was raised. "Very few people, with one hour of their day, one hour of their life—that's all the show was—can impact this many people," said Boys & Girls Clubs vice president Frank Sanchez.

Many people believed that LeBron's live, public announcement of his future plans was a hard way for his current team and fans—as well as the other teams hoping to sign him—to hear the news. What was typically done behind closed doors was happening in front of a live television audience. For months rumors had swirled about LeBron's future. Some people believed he was headed for Miami to join the Heat. Others thought he would end up with the New York Knicks. Shares of Madison Square Garden stock, the stadium where the Knicks play, rose in value based on the rumors. No one was sure where LeBron was headed.

USA TODAY Snapshots®

Most influential athletes

1. Lance Armstrong, cycling
2. LeBron James, basketball
3. Tim Tebow, football
4. Shaun White, extreme sports
5. Shaquille O'Neal, basketball

Source: Encino E-Poll Market Research via Forbes.com

By George Artsitas and Alejandro Gonzalez, USA TODAY, 2010

"This is the biggest play the league has seen since Michael Jordan retired and came back. I don't think people even understand the carry-down effect of what's going to happen," sports marketing expert Brandon Steiner said. LeBron's new team would see a huge increase in ticket and merchandise sales, and the whole area would benefit economically. "This is a function of our times," said basketball agent David Falk. "It's fun to watch the hoopla, but this is not a complex decision. . . . If I am LeBron, I have one question: Where can you win the most championships?"

LeBron was one of the best players in history to have not won a championship ring. While he always worked hard during his seven seasons in Cleveland, the burden of carrying the team by himself was becoming too much for him to handle. He was frustrated and ready for a change. Cleveland fans feared this meant they would lose both their top player and native son (LeBron was born near Cleveland in Akron, Ohio).

Attentive audience: LeBron *(left)* is surrounded by children at the Boys & Girls Club of America in Greenwich, Connecticut.

On the night of "The Decision," just minutes before the show's 9:00 P.M. broadcast, the Cavaliers were informed privately that LeBron would not return to the team. Instead, LeBron would join friends Dwyane Wade and Chris Bosh with the Miami Heat. "I'm going to take my talents to South Beach and join the Miami Heat . . . ," LeBron said during "The Decision." "I feel like it's going to give me the best opportunity to win and to win for multiple years, and not just to win in the regular season or just win five games in a row or three games in a row, I want to be able to win championships."

According to NBA rules, LeBron would receive less money from the Heat than he would have gotten from Cleveland, the team that drafted him. "For me, it's not about sharing. It's about . . . doing what's best for the team," LeBron said. And what of his beloved Cavaliers fans? "They['ve] seen me grow from an 18–year-old kid to a 25–year-old man," he said. "And I never wanted to leave Cleveland. And my heart will always be around that area." Whether his choice would prove to be right or wrong, LeBron had certainly come a long way from his humble beginnings.

Say cheese!: LeBron *(third row, center)* poses with officials and children from the Boys & Girls Clubs of America after his big 2010 announcement.

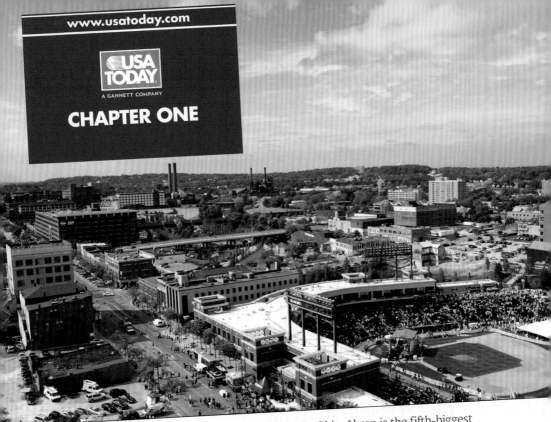

Hometown: LeBron was born and raised in Akron, Ohio. Akron is the fifth-biggest city in the state.

A Natural Athlete

LeBron Raymone James began life in a tough situation. He was born on December 30, 1984. His mother, Gloria James, was just 16 when LeBron was born. Unmarried and still in high school, Gloria struggled with her new baby. She lived with her mother, Freda, and her two younger brothers in a poor neighborhood in Akron, Ohio. Crime, such as gang and drug violence, was common on the streets.

Although LeBron has never met his real father, a man named Anthony McClelland, he has known the man he calls dad since he was a baby. Gloria met Eddie Jackson before her son's first birthday, and Freda allowed him to live with the family. Eddie was a troubled young man who was in and out of jail for much of LeBron's boyhood, but they still formed a strong bond.

Eddie and Gloria got LeBron a child-size basketball hoop for Christmas, just days before LeBron turned three. Right away, LeBron started slam-dunking the ball. Not even raising the hoop to its highest level could stop him. "Man, this kid has some elevation for just being three years old," Eddie said.

Sadly, just as LeBron was learning to love basketball, his grandmother died. Without Freda James, her daughter and sons found it too hard to pay the bills and keep their house. They were forced to split up and move in with friends and other family members. LeBron and Gloria stayed at different places for a few months at a time. By the time he was five, LeBron had moved seven times.

Despite the hardships, Gloria managed to keep her young son fed and clothed. But she knew LeBron needed more stability as he got older to help him stay off the streets and away from all the violence. With his natural athletic ability, sports seemed like a good way to keep LeBron out of trouble.

New Team, New Family

The first team sport LeBron played wasn't basketball. When he was nine years old, LeBron started playing football with the South Rangers, part of the Akron Parent Peewee Football Association. Right away, LeBron liked being part of a team. He liked the rules, learning plays, and making friends. He had lived in so many places and gone to so many schools, he didn't know many kids his own age with similar interests. LeBron liked the game so much that he decided he wanted to play in the National Football League (NFL) when he grew up.

Joining the South Rangers changed LeBron's life in other ways as well. His coach, Frankie Walker, knew about LeBron's hard family life.

Part of a team: LeBron began playing youth football for a team like the one shown here when he was nine years old.

In fourth grade, LeBron had often missed school and was in danger of being kicked out. The coach invited LeBron to live with the Walker family until LeBron's mother had a steady job and a home of her own. Knowing that this was what her son needed and that she could see him each weekend, Gloria agreed to the idea.

The Walkers had three children of their own, and all members of the family were big sports fans. In addition to football, Frankie coached a youth basketball team in Akron called the Summit Lake Hornets. Soon young LeBron joined the team and showed a natural talent on the basketball court. He was so impressive that by the end of his first season, Frankie asked LeBron if he wanted to help coach the younger kids. During his fifth-grade year, LeBron learned about being a role model to the younger boys. He worked hard to turn in his homework on time and have a good attitude on and off the court.

In 1995, after a year with the Walkers, LeBron began living with his mother again. Gloria had found a steady job and an apartment. But she continued to enforce the rules that the Walkers had used with

Future star: LeBron *(second from right)* hangs out with his youth basketball teammates.

LeBron. "He knows schoolwork comes first: no work, no basketball," Gloria said.

As he moved through middle school, football and basketball became bigger parts of LeBron's life. He worked hard to manage school, sports, and free time. LeBron played football in the fall and basketball all winter, spring, and summer. In addition, he had chores and homework. Like most boys, he also liked movies and video games. LeBron didn't mind his busy schedule. In fact, he thrived on it. And his basketball skills continued to improve. Passing, shooting, playing tough defense—LeBron could do it all on the court.

"I always knew that he would be real good, maybe a college scholarship player, but the revelation about the depth of his talent came when he was in eighth grade," Eddie Jackson later told *USA Today*. "That's when we knew he was given very special talents."

LeBron played for the Shooting Stars in middle school, a basketball team of the Amateur Athletic Union (AAU). The AAU is one of the largest nonprofit organized sports organizations in the world. Its focus is on amateur youth sports, with basketball being one of its most popular. LeBron quickly fell in with three other players: Dru Joyce III, Willie McGee, and Sian Cotton. Together with LeBron, the group called themselves the Fab Four. And sure enough, these four made magic happen on the court. "They believed in themselves and each other," Shooting Stars coach Dru Joyce II said.

The Fab Four's belief in one another as well as their precision in games led the team to multiple national championships and more than 200 wins in the years 1996–1999. As a member of the Shooting Stars, LeBron was able to compare himself to some of the best young teen players in the United States. He also got to travel around the country for the first time, an experience that was both exciting and scary. LeBron had never been on an airplane before! It was becoming clear that LeBron's talent was going to take him far.

High School Hopes

In Akron, students are allowed to choose which high school they attend. The Fab Four wanted to stay together. They chose Saint Vincent-Saint Mary (SVSM) High School, a small Catholic school. Their decision surprised many people who thought they would go to a bigger, more sports-oriented high school in the area. But LeBron and his teammates thought that SVSM was the best fit for them.

Saint Vincent-Saint Mary High School was formed in 1973 when Saint Vincent High School merged with Saint Mary High School.

LeBron entered his freshman year in 1999 at 6 feet 4 inches and 170 pounds. While he might have looked more like a basketball player, LeBron still played football that fall. Like his idol, NBA superstar Michael Jordan, LeBron showed that most elite athletes are talented at more than one sport. (In addition to basketball, Jordan played a season of professional baseball.) LeBron played wide receiver for SVSM and was moved up from the freshman to the varsity team midway through the season.

As soon as football season ended, basketball began. And what a freshman year it was for LeBron! That season the Fighting Irish (SVSM's nickname) were undefeated, winning all 27 games they played, thanks in large part to LeBron and the rest of

High school leader: LeBron *(above)* chose number 23 for his high school jersey to honor his hero, Michael Jordan. Jordan wore number 23 for most of his career.

the Fab Four. LeBron averaged 18 points and 6.2 rebounds per game. What was even more impressive was that while he was clearly a star on the court, LeBron was not a ball hog. He passed to teammates and looked for chances to let others shine. This made him as well liked by teammates as he was respected for his skills.

"He's very versatile and very unselfish. He could go into every game and pad his stats, but he wants to pass the ball, he wants to play a team game," said Dave Hoover, head basketball coach at McKinley Senior High School in Canton, Ohio, one of SVSM's opponents. "He just enjoys playing with friends."

It was no surprise when SVSM won the 1999–2000 Ohio State Boys Basketball Tournament. What was surprising was the huge crowd that came out to watch them win the championship. On March 25, 2000, over 13,000 fans saw SVSM beat Greeneview High School for the state title. LeBron and his teammates had become local stars.

The summer before his sophomore year of high school, LeBron played in a basketball tournament in California and a basketball camp in Pittsburgh. He impressed players and coaches alike with his skills and learned some of the finer points of the game he had grown to love. But basketball was still not the only sport for LeBron. He entered his sophomore year as the star wide receiver for the SVSM football team. LeBron took on the challenge, catching 42 passes that season and scoring 11 touchdowns. He was named All-Ohio first team.

The real excitement for LeBron started that November with basketball season. Once again, the Fighting Irish had one of the best high school teams in the country. With the addition of new player Romeo Travis, the Fab Four could now be called the Fab Five.

The season was going along smoothly for SVSM, with all wins and no losses, until they played Oak Hill Academy, the top-ranked high

The Fab Five: LeBron *(second from left)* poses with his SVSM teammates.

school team from Virginia. The game had to be played at nearby Ohio State University to seat the huge crowd of fans and media members who all wanted to see basketball's next superstar, LeBron James, take on one of the country's best high school teams.

SVSM led for the first two quarters. But in the game's second half, Oak Hill gained speed and cut the SVSM lead. In the game's final minutes, LeBron got a cramp and had to go to the bench. He returned to the court after a few minutes but missed several shots. Oak Hill won the game by a single point, 79–78. LeBron was disappointed in the loss, but he got right back to work on the court. His efforts helped lead SVSM to another state championship later that season.

LeBron was named to *USA Today*'s All-USA boys basketball team. He was also crowned Mr. Basketball of Ohio, a title given to the best amateur basketball player in the state. "It feels good to be recognized as the best sophomore in the country," 16-year-old LeBron said. "I think it stems from a combination of my being blessed with a lot of physical ability and my working hard. I don't want to be known as the best player in Akron or in Ohio. I want to be the best player in the country." While already famous in his hometown and surrounding areas for his incredible talent, LeBron was now starting to get national attention as well.

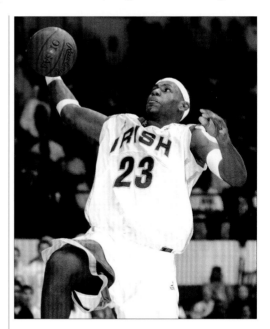

Mr. Basketball: His basketball skills made LeBron *(above)* one of the most famous athletes in Ohio.

USA TODAY
A GANNETT COMPANY

CHAPTER TWO

Budding superstar: LeBron (*above*) played at the ABCD Camp in 2001 with young basketball stars from around the country.

"The Chosen One"

LeBron began his junior year at SVSM in 2001 after a summer of basketball camps where he proved again that he was a force on the court. He teamed up with and played against the best players in the country at the USA Basketball Men's Youth Development Festival in Colorado and the ABCD Camp in New Jersey. At 6 feet 6 inches and 225 pounds, LeBron had the size to dominate a basketball game.

LeBron was respected on the football field as well as the basketball court, and he was proud that he played more than one sport. But Gloria James was beginning to worry that playing both basketball and football was too much for her son. While LeBron could have focused on football and possibly been a success in college and even the NFL, the NBA was his ultimate goal.

When LeBron fractured his finger during a football game, he realized that football injuries could threaten his basketball career. So despite scoring 11 touchdowns during the 2001–2002 season and helping his team to the playoffs, once football season ended, LeBron decided to focus only on basketball for the rest of his time in high school. Most people thought it was a good decision. "He's the best high school basketball player in the country, a great offensive talent," basketball analyst Van Coleman said. "He's 6'6" with a man's body. You want to see how good a guy is, don't watch him play against good opponents. Watch him against great opponents. This kid has outplayed some of the best players in the country."

In early 2002, *Sports Illustrated* ran a cover story about LeBron, calling him "The Chosen One." LeBron was the only high school junior the magazine had ever picked to grace its cover. Fans found him wherever he went, asking him to sign their magazine covers. But LeBron knew that some people would take advantage of his fame if they could. "Everybody comes up to me, all these grown folks, asking for autographs, talking about it's for their kids," LeBron said. "Next thing you know, they're selling it on eBay."

IN FOCUS

Akron, Ohio

Akron, Ohio, where LeBron was born, is located southeast of Cleveland. Just over 199,000 people live in Akron according to the 2010 census. The city used to be known as the Rubber Capital of the World.

Center of attention: By the early 2000s, LeBron *(center)* had become the most famous high school athlete in the country.

Instead of relaxing and enjoying his newfound national fame, LeBron concentrated on his game. While he improved on his already impressive career numbers during the 2001–2002 high school basketball season, averaging 29 points, 8.3 rebounds, and 5.3 assists per game, the team did not repeat as state champions. SVSM lost the championship game to Cincinnati's Roger Bacon High School. More than 18,000 fans had crowded into the stadium to watch the state championship game. LeBron took the loss hard, but he showed good sportsmanship by shaking hands with every player on the opposing team.

LeBron was once again named Ohio's Mr. Basketball and to *USA Today*'s All-USA boys basketball team after the 2001–2002 season. In addition, LeBron became Gatorade's National Basketball Player of the Year. LeBron had accomplished so much in just three high school basketball seasons that rumors began swirling that he was going to skip his senior year and enter the NBA draft. Other people said that LeBron might go to Europe and play professional basketball for millions of dollars a year. But LeBron's mother quickly squashed the rumors. "There has never been any plan other than for LeBron to finish up at St. V's. If he was going somewhere else, he'd be gone by now," Gloria James told reporters. "St. V's has been very good for him."

Looking Forward

With the promise of professional basketball money close at hand, it was hard for LeBron not to imagine being rich someday. He still lived in a modest apartment with his mother, and money was short. The idea of never having to worry about money again was exciting. But there are rules about amateur players and their *eligibility* to play after accepting cash or other gifts. During his high school years, LeBron was allowed to receive free items of clothing from sneaker company Adidas but little else. "We're glad he wears our clothes," said Adidas executive sports director Sonny Vaccaro. "We've already profited from him tenfold from what he's received. Everybody has profited from his celebrity— except him."

LeBron was invited to practice with the NBA's Cleveland Cavaliers in May 2002. He happily accepted. His remarkable basketball skills had Cleveland head coach John Lucas hoping for the sight of LeBron in a Cavaliers jersey someday soon. Unfortunately, the practice session broke the rule that

Coach in waiting: Former Cleveland Cavaliers coach John Lucas *(above)* caused trouble for himself and his team by contacting LeBron while the young player was still in high school.

December 13, 2002

Ohio teen doesn't disappoint ; High school phenom shows he has all the tools

From the Pages of
USA TODAY

CLEVELAND—Now everybody knows.

LeBron James is not a myth. He is as good as the hype. He proved it to a national television audience Thursday against USA TODAY's top-ranked high school team in the nation.

Forget the hoopla and the debates over if all this attention and exploitation should be heaped on a 17–year-old and just look forward to enjoy seeing him play in the NBA next season. He will be the surefire No. 1 overall pick in next June's draft, if he chooses to go directly to the NBA, which all indications are that he will.

"I talked to some scouts who I know and respect who have seen him, and they all say they'd like to see what he could do in a college situation, but they have no reservations about him making it big in the NBA," Bernie Bickerstaff says. "Patience is the thing, though. Remember, it took Kobe Bryant, Tracy McGrady and Kevin Garnett three years before they got the minutes and really made an impact."

One could take one look at Garnett, Bryant and McGrady when they were in high school and see that they were ready for the NBA. But they looked like high school kids, skinny and hyper. James looks like an NBA small forward. He has the NBA body, the NBA game and the NBA mind-set.

James had 31 points, 13 rebounds and six assists as his St. Vincent-St. Mary (Akron, Ohio) team, No. 23 in the USA TODAY Super 25 rankings, upset No. 1 Oak Hill Academy (Mouth of Wilson, Va.) 65–45. He dismantled the high

an NBA team cannot contact a player who is not eligible for the draft. The Cavaliers were fined $150,000, and Lucas was suspended for the first two games of the season.

school power that features five future Division I players and has lost just six games in five years.

The numbers don't tell the whole story with James, though, it's the overall impression, the maturity, the demeanor and the ease at which he handles all of the pressure that sets him apart.

"Some of the things he does remind me of McGrady," says Bickerstaff, who has worked for the Washington Wizards, Seattle SuperSonics and Denver Nuggets and is a consultant for the Harlem Globetrotters. "The way he moves and passes off the dribble."

Not only was this the first time in 13 years ESPN has televised a regular-season high school basketball game, but also the Goodyear blimp, for the first time in its 77 years in the air, was overhead at a high school basketball game. Representatives from 10 NBA teams and a host of representatives from Nike and Adidas were also present.

Walking the walk: LeBron used to wear a leg band on the court that said "Chosen One."

"I hope Kobe is watching," James says before the game.

Comparing James to anybody is dangerous so early in his career.

"He should just go out to be the best LeBron James he can be," Bickerstaff says. "The test results are already in on Michael and Kobe and those guys, and they passed. This is LeBron James, and he has to do things his way."

James is expected to make three times as much with his first shoe contract as he is with his first NBA contract. He wore Nikes in his last game and in this game wore specially-made Adidas shoes in the first half and switched to the same Adidas' his teammates wore in the second half.

—David DuPree

LeBron broke his wrist during a dunk in the summer of 2002. While he healed in just eight weeks, the injury led Gloria to take out an insurance policy on her son. LeBron's NBA career could have been over before it had even begun if the break had been more severe.

The hype surrounding LeBron was bigger than ever at the beginning of the 2002–2003 season, his final year at SVSM. Everyone was wondering where LeBron would end up after high school, but most suspected he would skip college and go straight to the NBA. LeBron had previously asked the NBA to change their rules about needing to graduate from high school before entering the draft, but his request was turned down.

The turnout for SVSM games was so large in 2002–2003 that all of their games had to be moved to the nearby University of Akron. NBA players like Shaquille O'Neal came to watch, and some games were even shown on ESPN. LeBron's national television debut was December 12, 2002. SVSM defeated archrival Oak Hill, 65–45. LeBron had an amazing 31 points, 13 rebounds, and six assists. The cameras, the crowd, and the victory made LeBron feel on top of the world.

USA TODAY Snapshots®

Shaq among the best

Shaquille O'Neal is 11th in NBA history in total points scored and within reach of the top 10. Active leaders in career points:

Shaquille O'Neal	**26,384**
Allen Iverson	**23,078**
Kobe Bryant	**21,741**
Kevin Garnett	**20,501**
Ray Allen	**18,351**
Tim Duncan	**17,926**

Through Monday
Source: basketball-reference.com

By Matt Eppers and Veronica Salazar, USA TODAY, 2008

Lessons Learned

LeBron's good fortune continued when he turned 18 on December 30, 2002, and received two very special gifts. The first was the announcement of *USA Today*'s ranking of the top high school basketball teams in the country. SVSM was number one! LeBron's second gift was a brand-new car from his mother. But it was not just any car—the gift was a luxury black and platinum Hummer H2 complete with three

Nice ride: LeBron poses with his Hummer H2, a gift from his mother.

TVs, a video game system, a DVD player, and personalized leather seats that read "King James."

Immediately, people began to wonder how Gloria, a poor woman living in a small apartment, could afford to buy an $80,000 car. Some people believed it was actually a gift from a big company trying to get LeBron to endorse its products after he graduated in the spring. Hummergate, as the scandal was called, was over as soon as Gloria showed paperwork proving she was making payments on the car. If it had been a gift from a company, LeBron would probably have been suspended for the remainder of his senior year.

Just a couple of weeks later, LeBron got into real trouble when he accepted two vintage sports jerseys from a local store owner in exchange for autographed photos. LeBron was suspended for two games. The team was also forced to forfeit one of their wins, which turned out to be SVSM's only loss that year. LeBron was very apologetic for his mistake and its effect on his team. "There's nothing I'm more sorry about ... [than] disrespecting my teammates ... ," LeBron said. "I love them to death and can do nothing without my teammates."

When LeBron returned after his short absence, he scored a personal high of 52 points in one game! It was no surprise that the team neared the end of the season with an 18–1 record and another shot at the state championship. In his final game as a high school player, LeBron and his SVSM teammates faced Archbishop Alter High School of Kettering, Ohio. Although SVSM was expected to win easily, LeBron

recalled his team's heart-wrenching loss in the 2002 state tournament. He did not want to lose another chance at the state title. The 2003 championship game was tight, but in the end, SVSM won, 40–36.

To honor LeBron, SVSM retired his jersey (number 23) and hung it from the rafters of the school's gym. It was a nice tribute to a player who finished his high school career with 2,657 points, 892 rebounds, and 523 assists. Once again, LeBron made *USA Today*'s All-USA

Take back the court: LeBron *(left)* returned after his suspension in 2003 to dominate the rest of the season.

LeBron had a lot of basketball talent, but he knew that he would have to work hard to develop his skills. In high school, he improved his game by shooting up to 800 jump shots every day at practice.

basketball team and was named Mr. Basketball of Ohio for the third time.

In April 2003, LeBron played in three high school all-star events: the McDonald's All-American Game, the EA Sports Roundball Classic, and the Capital Classic. He was voted Most Valuable Player (MVP) at each game. By playing in more than two of these events where NBA scouts are present, LeBron lost his eligibility to play in the National Collegiate Athletic Association (NCAA). This meant LeBron was headed for the NBA! On April 25, 2003, he announced to the world that he was entering the NBA draft.

Retired: Fans cheer as LeBron holds his framed jersey in 2003. No SVSM basketball players will wear number 23 after LeBron.

The NBA draft is held each year and consists of two rounds. Sixty new players are chosen by teams during the draft from a pool of eligible participants.

The 2003 NBA draft was held on June 26 and the Cleveland Cavaliers had the first choice. Not surprisingly, Ohio native LeBron was their pick. The Cavaliers 2002–2003 record was a dismal 17 wins and 65 losses. Once they scored LeBron, Cavs fans were hopeful for a playoff spot the next season. Eighteen-year-old LeBron was a little more realistic about his upcoming rookie year. "There may be some people out there [expecting that], but the real people who know basketball know that's impossible . . . ," he said. "I hope they will see that we're a better team than we were the year before and next year we're a better team than we were this year, that we're progressing."

LeBron played less basketball than he had in years during the summer after graduation. His life was too busy with business deals and travel.

Newest Cavalier: LeBron *(right)* shakes hands with NBA commissioner David Stern after LeBron was chosen with the first pick in the 2003 NBA draft.

Getting started: LeBron shoots the ball as new Cavaliers coach Paul Silas looks on during a practice before the 2003-2004 NBA season.

He was asked to go on talk shows and do interviews. And he spent as much time as he could with his friends. LeBron even treated his friends to a trip to Los Angeles and paid for it all.

LeBron did find time to think about his future during the summer of 2003. He knew the game would be harder in the NBA. He was used to going up against high school boys, but in the NBA, he would face men who were bigger and had more experience. LeBron knew by working hard, he could compete with anyone. As the 2003–2004 NBA season neared, LeBron's fans were anxious to see if the high school sensation would turn into a professional star.

In the Spotlight: LeBron speaks with reporters in June 2003.

Rookie of the Year

Before he even took the court for his first professional basketball game with the Cleveland Cavaliers, LeBron was already a multimillionaire. He signed a deal to endorse Nike that was estimated at $90 million. He had a $5 million deal with sports and entertainment company Upper Deck, and an $11 million, 3-year contract with the Cavaliers. "My life hasn't changed," LeBron insisted. "I just have a little bit more money now. I'm still the same old person I was before."

NIKE

Founded near Portland, Oregon, in 1972 by Phil Knight and Bill Bowerman, Nike is one of the biggest athletic apparel organizations in the world. The company employs more than 35,000 people on six continents.

LeBron quickly got the chance to prove he was the same person on the basketball court. On October 29, 2003, LeBron dazzled the huge number of reporters and fans on hand at ARCO Arena in Sacramento, California. The Cavaliers faced the Sacramento Kings. Although the Cavaliers lost the game, LeBron scored 25 points, made 9 assists, grabbed 6 rebounds, and had 4 steals. It was an impressive start to his professional career.

LeBron turned nineteen on December 30. It was hard to believe that he was still a teenager, but he seemed ready to live up to the hype that always surrounded him. New Cavaliers coach Paul Silas was impressed by LeBron's work ethic and how well he took criticism to improve his play. "I just mentioned a few things on the court, and he accepted them and did them," Coach Silas said. "That shows he loves the game and wants to play the game. That's important. He's humble. His humility will make him fit in better. He's really aware of where he is and how he has to fit in. That's going to bode well for him."

On March 27, 2004, LeBron and the Cavaliers faced the New Jersey Nets in Cleveland. LeBron was off his game in the first quarter, scoring only two points. But he started to play better after that. The two teams were tied, 96–96, in the middle of the final quarter, thanks in large part to LeBron's play. Then, in the final two minutes of the game, LeBron scored an incredible 10 points. The final score was Cleveland 107, New Jersey 104.

December 30, 2003

Shockingly, Cavaliers rookie James lives up to hyperbole

From the Pages of
USA TODAY

LeBron James turns 19 today, and what would Friedrich Melchior von Grimm have written about that? The 18th-century French author once said this about a prodigy [talent] born too soon to score a $90 million Nike deal: "He has shown me how difficult it is to preserve one's sanity in the face of a miracle."

Yes, [composer] Wolfgang Mozart had game, too. In fact, young Mozart might be the last teenager to do anything as perfectly as young James plays basketball. On their 19th birthdays, Tiger Woods didn't putt like this, Lance Armstrong didn't pedal like this, Muhammad Ali didn't punch like this and Michael Jordan sure didn't pass like this.

So James is another Magic Johnson or Larry Bird? Come on, LeBron has more athletic ability in his right pinkie toe than Magic and Bird had on their best gravity-challenged day. Don't rely on box scores to tell you James has reached a rookie summit never approached by Kobe Bryant, Kevin Garnett, Tracy McGrady and every other teen wonder who shook David Stern's hand.

Watch how LeBron plays point guard for the Cleveland Cavaliers, handling the Scottie Pippen role for the first three quarters before seizing the Jordan role in the fourth. Listen to his coach, Paul Silas, describe how LeBron studies grainy footage from the NBA's Jurassic Age. "One day he was talking about how (Bill) Laimbeer shot the ball with the step forward," Silas said. "Who would've thought a kid his age would even know about Bill Laimbeer?"

Who would've thought James would be a role model for players twice his age?

"At 18," said new Cavs teammate Eric Williams, "the poise to be that unselfish is amazing."

James just managed 32 points, 10 rebounds and nine assists in a victory against the Trail Blazers, who scored eight fourth-quarter points to LeBron's 12. This is becoming a nightly bulletin, even with the Cavs at 10–21. The Boston trade changed everything. James is so much better without serial loser Ricky Davis and with team-firsters Williams and Tony Battie, men who have no problem with the fact a child must lead them.

"They know I'm a natural born leader," LeBron said. "I've been a leader my whole life, and that comes from being an only child."

James said this after ringing up 36 to a few hysterical chants of "O-ver-ra-ted" in Philadelphia, setting the NBA record for points on the road by a teenager and starting his run of four 30–plus scoring performances in six games. Absorbing LeBron's presence from courtside that night it was hard to believe his previous game in Philly came against Strawberry Mansion High at the Scholastic Play-by-Play Classic.

But while James stretched his Greek sculpture of a body across his locker room floor before that Sixers game, he confirmed as much by discussing this year's crop of big-name high school seniors who might take the LeBron LeLeap. "Dwight something," he said of the Southwest Atlanta Christian center. "Dwight Howard," I answered. "I think Sebastian (Telfair) and Shaun Livingston might come out," James added, before agreeing that Josh Smith, Al Jefferson and Robert Swift were among the other prom-to-the-pros possibilities.

"There's not going to be anyone left in high school," James said through a smile. "I was fortunate. The Cavs had the No. 1 pick, and they just liked me because I lived 30 minutes away in Akron. I don't know why they picked me. I can't play basketball."

James plays it like American kids aren't supposed to. His is a fundamental genius supposedly cornered by the European market but on display in the form of the next No. 1 pick. Howard, the son of a Georgia state trooper, wowed 17 NBA scouts at Delaware's Slam Dunk to the Beach tournament the other night with 25 points, 21 rebounds, nine blocks, five assists and one frightening ability to handle the ball on the break.

"If I go pro I'm thinking I'm going in there to dominate right away," Howard said in his locker room. "What I want to do is . . . show everybody LeBron just set a standard for high schoolers that we can play basketball with the big boys. . . . I think I can surpass LeBron."

If it sounds crazy, so did the notion of James standing among the 10 or 12 best players in the NBA. Howard's next tour stop is Saturday's Pangos Dream Classic at UCLA, while James will continue to sell $110 sneakers and make the kind of beautiful music worthy of a Mozart in shorts.

"So premature a fruit might fall before it has come to maturity," Friedrich Melchior von Grimm warned about young Wolfgang. Even ol' Freddy wouldn't have sweated young LeBron's fate. The kid shares Michael Jordan's number and Tiger Woods' birthday, but James rose this morning as a 19–year-old prodigy beyond modern-day compare.

—Ian O'Connor

Record breaker: LeBron *(center)* goes to the basket for two of the 41 points he scored against the New Jersey Nets on March 27, 2004.

This game was more than just a win for the Cavaliers, it was record making for LeBron. With his 41 points, he became the youngest player in NBA history to score more than 40 points in a single game. Few people were surprised when LeBron was named NBA Rookie of the Year a month later. He was the youngest player to ever win the award and the first Cavalier. In his acceptance speech, LeBron was humble, thanking his mother, coach, and Cavaliers teammates for his success.

LeBron had come a long way in a short time in the NBA, but he still remembered the help he got when he and his mother were struggling. He wanted to give back. LeBron spoke to groups of children, encouraging them to follow their dreams and to work hard to get there. But he knew that it took more than just a dream when you have nothing. In 2004 LeBron and his mother founded the LeBron James Family Foundation to teach children to be physically fit, academically focused, and environmentally aware and to help single-parent families in need.

Award winner: LeBron *(left)* is shown here accepting the Rookie of the Year award for the 2003–2004 NBA season.

The foundation sponsors charity events to support groups such as the YMCA and the Akron Urban League. LeBron appears at many of the events to help raise money.

Olympics and Fatherhood

The USA Men's National Basketball Team has a history of taking home the gold medal at the Olympic Games. In 2004 LeBron became the youngest player to be chosen for the team since 1968. LeBron was flattered and excited to travel to Athens, Greece, for the Summer Olympic Games. The first modern Olympic Games were held in Athens in 1896. But Team USA's head coach, Larry Brown, relied on his more experienced players. LeBron didn't play a lot, averaging just over 14 minutes a game with 5.8 points and 2.6 rebounds.

Overseas: LeBron played well in limited minutes during the Olympic Games in Athens, Greece, in 2004.

The team returned home to the United States with a bronze medal. The third-place finish was a disappointment. Many people criticized the players for their big egos and for not playing as a team. Some people pointed out that Olympic basketball games had different rules than the NBA. Maybe the new rules caused the team to not play as well as they could. Others thought Coach Brown didn't play his younger players like LeBron often enough. Despite not winning the gold medal, LeBron enjoyed his two weeks in Greece and being a part of the biggest sports competition in the world.

After he returned home in August, LeBron got to work to prepare for his upcoming second season with the Cavaliers. "I didn't play much in the Olympics," LeBron said. "I had a lot of energy when I got back, and I was ready to just get back to my teammates." But basketball wasn't the only thing on LeBron's mind at this time. He was going to be a father! LeBron's longtime sweetheart from high school, Savannah Brinson, gave birth to son LeBron James Jr. on October 6, 2004.

Unlike his own birth father, LeBron vowed to always be there for his son. While many worried that he was too young to be a good parent, LeBron was ready for more responsibility both on and off the court.

And there was no doubt he could afford to support a family financially. The proud father even got a tattoo on his arm of his son's face.

With the addition to his family, LeBron had even more motivation to play well in his second season with the Cavaliers. He had a new son to cheer him on. And the Cavaliers looked like a different team during the 2004–2005 preseason, winning six of their eight games. Cleveland fans were hoping that this was the year the team made a turnaround and went to the playoffs for the first time since 1998.

Winning Season

LeBron was eager for the 2004–2005 season to begin and was determined not to fall into a sophomore slump. Sophomore slump is the nickname given to a player's second season that is less impressive than his or her first. When the regular season began, LeBron and the

USA TODAY Snapshots®

Still searching for a championship

The Sacramento Kings, seeded sixth in the NBA playoffs, have waited more than half a century to win an NBA title. Teams that have gone the longest without winning the NBA championship:

Sacramento Kings	Atlanta Hawks	Phoenix Suns	Cleveland Cavaliers	Los Angeles Clippers
53 years	46	36	34	34

Source: AP

By Ellen J. Horrow and Robert W. Ahrens, USA TODAY, 2005

Cavs did seem to struggle for wins, but they quickly rallied and ended November with a 9–5 record.

The Cavaliers' good play was due in no small part to LeBron's versatility on the court. "Listed as a small forward, [LeBron] has a point guard's mentality and the skills of a shooting guard, power forward, and center," sports reporter David DuPree wrote. "He goes to his left as well as his right and usually gets there with ease, even though every defense is designed to keep him away from the basket."

Keeping LeBron from the basket was no easy task in the 2004–2005 season. He seemed to be able to do whatever he wanted to do on the court. The 20-year-old became the youngest player in history to record a triple-double in an NBA game, meaning he racked up double-digit totals in three statistical categories. LeBron's 27 points, 11 rebounds, and 10 assists lead the Cavaliers to their 23rd win of the season. "I knew he was going to improve, but just how much, I didn't know," Coach Silas said. "He's really something now . . . he is just spectacular at times. But he's totally within himself, and that's the amazing part to me, that he's grasped his things so quickly, and understands so much about his role and how he fits."

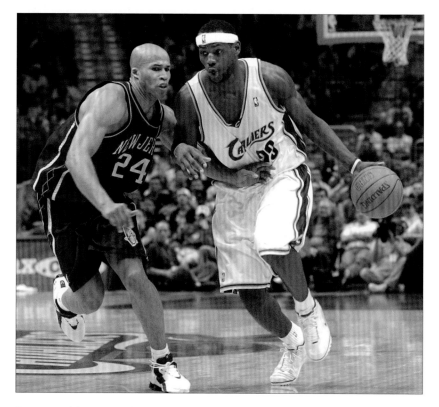

Unstoppable: LeBron *(right)* is often bigger and stronger than the players trying to guard him.

Masked man: Wearing a clear, protective mask didn't seem to bother LeBron (*above*) on the court.

LeBron seemed to be settling into a leadership role with the Cavs. But the day before his 20th birthday, LeBron's season could have come to an end. He collided with Houston Rockets center Dikembe Mutombo and suffered a broken cheekbone. Towering over most NBA players, Mutombo is 7 feet 2 inches (2.19 meters) and 260 pounds (117.9 kilograms). The accident forced LeBron to sit out the next game. He returned in early January wearing a clear mask to protect his injured cheek during play. Despite the distraction of the mask, LeBron continued to play at his best and was named to his first NBA All-Star Game. The All-Star Game is a basketball-fan favorite in which the best and most popular players in the Eastern Conference and the Western Conference are chosen to compete against each other by fan votes as well as by NBA coaches.

The first NBA All-Star Game was held in 1951. The Eastern Conference beat the Western Conference, 111–94.

In March 2005, the Cavaliers traveled to Canada to play the Toronto Raptors. Cleveland had faced a series of losses, and the team needed a win. Perhaps no one was more eager to get back on the right track that night than LeBron. He was focused and intense and with 56 points on the night, he became the youngest player in NBA history to score more than 50 points in a single game. Still, LeBron's efforts came up short when the Cavs lost, 107–98. Despite that he had scored more than half of the Cavs' 98 points, LeBron was disappointed by the outcome of the game.

LeBron's 2004–2005 season averages of 27.2 points, 7.2 assists, 7.4 rebounds, and 2.2 steals per game were impressive. And his four triple-doubles, 27 games with 30 or more points, five with 40 or more, and one with more than 50 were jaw-dropping. But what LeBron wanted most was victory for his team, not personal glory. Even though the team had its first winning season in seven years with a 42–40 record, they failed to get a playoff spot.

Two-way player: LeBron *(top)* is known for his impressive offensive skills, but he is also a talented defender.

By now LeBron was being compared to some of basketball's biggest names, such as Shaquille O'Neal, Michael Jordan, Kobe Bryant, and Dwyane Wade. But what all of these players had that LeBron did not was at least one NBA championship. He was determined that next season was going to be his team's year.

Before the 2004–2005 season had ended, Coach Silas was fired due to conflict with the team's new owner, Dan Gilbert. Some thought Silas's sudden departure would be hard on the team and LeBron in particular. General Manager Jim Paxson was also fired.

Another big change was in store for LeBron at this time. He parted ways with Aaron and Eric Goodwin, his agents of almost two years. To replace them, LeBron hired close childhood friend Maverick Carter from SVSM, who was just 23 years old at the time, to manage his business deals. Critics said the choice was foolish, that Carter was too young and inexperienced. But, as he had for years, LeBron trusted his instincts.

New manager: Maverick Carter (*above*) began representing LeBron in 2005. Carter is the cofounder of marketing company LRMR.

Despite all the fanfare surrounding him after two years in the NBA, LeBron remained humble. "LeBron has an ability to stay grounded even amidst the uproar and expectation that is around him," said Rodney Knox, Nike's director of communications. "As opposed to being overwhelmed, he embraces it and enjoys it. He wants to be a role model and to succeed, and he doesn't feel that it's any pressure. He welcomes a lot of things that would be a burden for others." LeBron did not feel burdened, but he knew it was time for his team to make the playoffs.

Heads together: Head coach Mike Brown (*left*) hoped that LeBron's talent would carry the team to a winning season.

A Rocky Road

■■■■■

With all the changes in the Cavaliers' front office, basketball fans were wondering if the team could put together a winning season in 2005–2006. New head coach Mike Brown knew that Cavs fans had been waiting to make it to the playoffs since 1998. They all knew that with LeBron on the team, there was a chance of making it. LeBron boldly predicted that the Cavaliers would have at least 50 wins.

The home opener on November 2,

2005, showed everyone that LeBron's prediction could very well come true. His three-point shooting took center stage that night. He hit five in a row and six total in the game. The Cavaliers took down the New Orleans Hornets, 109–87. It was a decisive win, and the victories kept coming.

On November 13, 2005, LeBron took to the court to play the Orlando Magic knowing he was just 10 points shy of reaching 4,000 career points. His 4,000th point came near the end of the first quarter, making him

Improvement: Cleveland fans were hopeful that LeBron (*above*) and the Cavs would be able to claim a playoff spot in 2005–2006.

the youngest player ever to hit this milestone. But there was little time to celebrate. LeBron was more interested in getting the win than in upping his personal point total. LeBron's teammate Donyell Marshall clinched the game that night, hitting a three-pointer with just seconds to play. The game was everything LeBron could have wished for: a win for his team, glory for a teammate, and a new record for himself!

The season was on the right track for the Cavaliers as they headed into 2006. Twenty-one-year-old LeBron was certain his team was where they needed to be to clinch a playoff spot. While he was the undeniable star of the team, other players were also at the top of their

USA TODAY Snapshots®

Active NBA players with most minutes played in a season

Kobe Bryant, L.A. Lakers	(2002-03)	**3,401**
Antawn Jamison, Golden State	(2000-01)	**3,394**
LeBron James, Cleveland	(2004-05)	**3,388**
Gilbert Arenas, Washington	(2005-06)	**3,384**
Shawn Marion, Phoenix	(2002-03)	**3,373**

Source: Basketball-Reference.com

By Kevin Greer and Sam Ward, USA TODAY, 2011

All-Star star: LeBron holds his MVP award after the 2005–2006 NBA All-Star Game.

games and the group was playing well together.

On February 19, LeBron played in his second All-Star Game, held at the Toyota Center in Houston, Texas. LeBron led his Eastern Conference teammates to a 122–120 victory over the Western Conference. With 29 points, 6 rebounds, and 2 assists, LeBron was the clear choice for MVP of the game. He was the youngest player to ever win this honor. LeBron showed his age by enthusiastically taking off his Nike sneakers and having his teammates sign them. He came to the postgame press conference wearing socks but no shoes!

Nike, of course, was thrilled with the attention given to their sneakers. Their advertising campaign with LeBron was paying off in a big way, and three sneakers bearing LeBron's name had already been released. LeBron was also featured in television and print commercials for Nike.

The Playoffs

While the All-Star Game had been fun for LeBron, his main focus was on helping his team finally get back to the playoffs. On April 19, 2006, LeBron was forced to sit out a nail-biting game against the Atlanta Hawks after spraining his ankle. Although LeBron's teammates missed him on the court, they managed to win by a single point and clinch a spot in the playoffs. And true to LeBron's prediction, the Cavs ended their season with 50 wins and 32 losses.

On the bench: LeBron *(left)* missed the final game of the 2005–2006 season. His injury wasn't serious, and he returned to the court a few days later for the playoffs.

March 13, 2006

Nike ads play on James' youthful exuberance

From the Pages of USA TODAY

NBA superstar LeBron James became the league's youngest All-Star MVP when he took the honor Feb. 19.

The 21–year-old plays like a veteran, but he shows a youthful exuberance off the court. Just moments after being named MVP, he removed his Nike Zoom shoes to have them autographed by his winning East teammates. The boyish feat left the Cleveland Cavaliers guard in stocking feet for the postgame press conference.

He also shows off his youthful enthusiasm in recent Nike ads. In the commercials, James portrays four dimensions of his personality on and off the court: youth, wisdom, business and athleticism.

Those are some of the same traits that landed James an estimated $90 million, seven-year Nike endorsement deal that runs through 2009. With that and other deals he has signed, he's now the No. 2 sports endorser behind Tiger Woods, also a Nike star.

Sports marketing expert David Paro says James is at the top of his game in the ads and on the court.

"He's doing his part living up to the hype," says Paro, president of Deep Alliance Marketing in Clarendon Hills, Ill.

"The guy can play. And when you have a guy like that, the person becomes big enough to become multidimensional. He's very good in those ads at playing each of the roles."

LeBron was thrilled for his team, and his own accomplishments that season were also impressive. He was named NBA Player of the Week for three weeks in a row and finished second to Phoenix's Steve Nash in voting

In the ads, James portrays each of the traits as characters who live together as the imaginary family of LeBrons. The wisdom character is the family patriarch. The business persona is the slick, hard-driving dealmaker. The athletic LeBron is the pro-hoops star. The child represents LeBron's enthusiasm. The characters eat, banter about sports and break into dance as the Rick James song "Super Freak" plays.

The ad storyline was developed by Nike and longtime ad agency Wieden & Kennedy in Portland, Ore., with James' help.

"It's not unlike how we develop any of our stories on our athletes," says Adam Roth, Nike ad director. "It's a pretty collaborative effort between ourselves, the agency and the athlete. We talk to the athlete and try to gain an authentic insight that maybe goes a little deeper than the world at large is seeing."

Nike tries to find an untold story by brainstorming with the Wieden ad folks in or around the sport that's being marketed. For the James ad, for instance, one of the first meetings took place on a basketball court where they played and talked.

The ad ideas were presented to James, who offered feedback and ideas before signing off on them.

The ads promote the third edition of the James basketball shoe: Zoom LeBron III. The shoe was released in November in black, white and red, and Nike already has added three more color schemes. Another is due April 1.

The shoe barely appears in the ads, but that was fine with consumers surveyed by Ad Track, USA TODAY's weekly poll.

Of those familiar with the ads, 20% like the ads a lot compared with the Ad Track average of 21%. They were a bigger hit with the key younger consumers—31% of 18– to 24–year-olds like the ads "a lot."

The prime target, Roth says: "Kids who play basketball. We go after that younger player, the teen baller."

But he says, with an "athlete of LeBron's scope, we're trying to appeal to a broader audience."

—Theresa Howard

for NBA MVP. He joined Kobe Bryant and his idol Michael Jordan as the only players since 1970 to score 35 points or more in 9 straight games. LeBron averaged 31.4 points, 7 rebounds, and 6.6 assists per game for the season.

First playoff series: LeBron *(center)* puts up a shot against the Washington Wizards.

On April 22, the Cavaliers faced the Washington Wizards in the first game of a seven-game playoff series. It was LeBron's playoff debut, and he was on fire, racking up a triple-double. The final score of the game was Cavaliers 97, Wizards 86. The teams traded victories over the next three games to tie the series at two each. Game Five was pivotal, and as usual, LeBron was determined to lead his team to victory.

The game was close from beginning to end, and the two teams traded the lead back and forth. Then, with just three seconds left in the game, LeBron got the ball near the basket and dodged three Wizards defenders to score the game-winning layup! "If I wore an eighteen- or nineteen-size shoe, I wouldn't have made it," LeBron joked after the win. "But I wear a sixteen and was able to tightrope that baseline to get a layup."

The Cavaliers won the next game and took the series. They next faced the Detroit Pistons in the Eastern Conference Semifinals. Unfortunately for the Cavs, the defending Eastern Conference champion Pistons had one of the best defenses in the league. They set to work on LeBron, preventing him from shooting as much as possible, and

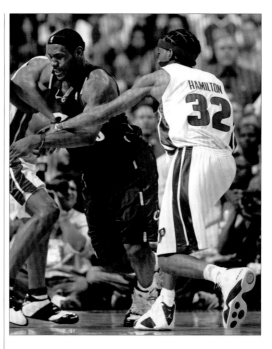

Smothered: Detroit Pistons guard Richard Hamilton *(right)* and his teammates work hard to shut down LeBron *(center)*.

triple-teamed him at times. The strategy worked, and the Pistons won the series, four games to three. Despite the heartbreaking loss, LeBron had played well, averaging 30.8 points, 8.1 rebounds, and 5.8 assists per game in the playoffs.

Another Chance

After the 2005–2006 season's end, LeBron took to the negotiating table with the Cavaliers. They added three years to his contract starting in the 2007–2008 season with the option to become an unrestricted free agent after the 2009–2010 season. An unrestricted free agent can sign with any team offering a contract. LeBron was happy with the Cavaliers and still had much to accomplish with the team. But he wanted to keep his options wide open for the future.

> ⓘ LeBron knows that nutrition is important to his performance on the court, and he follows a strict diet. He usually eats about three hours before game time.

That summer LeBron joined many of his former Olympic teammates when he traveled to Japan to play in the International Basketball Federation (FIBA) World Championship. Once again, Team USA took home the bronze medal, finishing behind Spain (gold) and Greece (silver). But with his 13.9 points, 4.8 rebounds, and 4.1 assists per game, LeBron did his best for the team.

LeBron was determined to also do his best in the upcoming 2006–2007 NBA season. Coach Brown decided that LeBron should go easy in the preseason so he could be rested and ready for the regular season, which started in November. With LeBron on the bench, the preseason wasn't pretty for the Cavs. But the regular season began with a win over the tough Washington Wizards. The months that followed had ups and downs for the Cavs, but they were looking as strong, if not stronger, than the season before. LeBron was doing his best to live up to the high expectations everyone had for him. "Everybody keeps asking for more, and he is a willing guy," Coach Brown said. "He just keeps giving us more."

LeBron gave it his all at the 2007 NBA All-Star Game where he scored 28 points in 32 minutes. But even better, the Cavs continued to win after the All-Star break and finished the season with a 50–32 record. The team was headed to the playoffs once again.

Just like the year before, first up for the Cavs in the playoffs were the Washington Wizards. But unlike 2006, the Cavaliers swept the Wizards in 2007, winning the first four games of the series to advance to the next level.

Beating the Nets: LeBron dribbles the ball against Jason Kidd of the New Jersey Nets. LeBron scored 30 points in the game.

Next up were the New Jersey Nets. While tougher to beat than the Wizards, the Cavs managed to win the series four games to two. After the Nets, the Cavs faced the Detroit Pistons in the Eastern Conference Finals. That team had knocked Cleveland out of the playoffs the year before. The Cavaliers were determined to make amends for the previous year's loss and make it to the NBA Finals.

The Pistons took the first game, and LeBron was criticized for the final seconds of his team's loss. He passed the ball to teammate Donyell Marshall, who missed a game-winning shot. Critics claimed LeBron should have taken the shot himself instead of passing to a teammate. People began to question LeBron's ability to lead his team to victory during the pressure-filled final moments of big games. But LeBron did not regret his decision, despite the loss. "I'm still the same player I was before all this happened," LeBron said. "If the game is close and I get double-teamed, I'm going to pass to the open man. . . . I'm the leader of this team, and I take credit when we win and I'll take [the blame]

Game winner: LeBron *(above)* splits the Pistons defense to score the winning basket in the second overtime of Game Five of the 2006–2007 Eastern Conference Finals.

when we [lose], too." The Pistons won the second game of the series before LeBron and the Cavaliers rallied to win the next two games. With the series tied, Cleveland took to the court for Game Five with confidence.

The game was close from beginning to end. With just 20 seconds left and Detroit up by two points, LeBron hit a shot to tie the game and send it into overtime. The score was tied again, 100–100, at the end of the first overtime. LeBron was on fire, answering each of the Pistons' baskets with one of his own. But near the end of the second overtime, it looked as though the Pistons would win as they were up by three. Then LeBron hit a three-pointer to tie the game again. Would the game go to a third overtime?

With just 11 seconds left to play, the Cavaliers got the ball back and called a timeout. Everyone knew that they were talking about how to get the ball to LeBron, who had scored all of Cleveland's points in the second overtime. With just two seconds remaining in the game, LeBron attacked the basket, dodged the Pistons' defense, and scored the game-winning layup! The Cavs' best player had come through when his team needed him most, scoring 48 points in the game. Even more impressive, LeBron had scored 29 of Cleveland's final 30 points. "Somebody told me in the locker room that he scored 29 of our last 30 points and I could not believe it," Coach Brown said. ESPN would later rate LeBron's play in this game as the fourth-best NBA playoff performance ever.

LeBron played well again in Game Six with 20 points and 14 rebounds. Cleveland took the game, 98–82, and won the series. In just four years, LeBron had helped transform one of the worst teams in the NBA to one of the best. The Cavaliers were going to the NBA Finals!

The Cleveland Cavaliers got their nickname from a Cleveland resident named Jerry Tomko. In 1970 the team held a contest to allow fans to suggest nicknames for the city's new NBA franchise, and Tomko suggested Cavaliers. He won the contest, and the team has been known as the Cavaliers ever since.

The Finals: LeBron (*right*) throws up a jump shot during Game One of the 2006–2007 NBA Finals.

King James

The Cavaliers were set to face the San Antonio Spurs for the 2007 NBA championship. As usual, all eyes were on LeBron and hopes were high in Cleveland. But it was not meant to be.

The Cavaliers struggled in Game One, losing 85–76, and in Game Two, losing 103–92. In Game Three, LeBron missed a three-pointer that could have sent the game into overtime. The final score was San Antonio 75, Cleveland 72. Despite

LeBron's many outstanding late-game performances in the past, there was more talk after the third loss to San Antonio that he didn't perform well at the end of important games. Some people thought the pressure of these moments was sometimes too much for LeBron to handle. But the 22–year-old forward had scored 25 points in the game, including 12 in the fourth quarter. People close to LeBron wondered what more he could do to help the team.

Swept: LeBron was disappointed after losing Game Four of the Finals. The Cavaliers were outplayed by the Spurs.

San Antonio won Game Four by a single point, 83–82, and took the NBA Finals. LeBron was devastated to have gotten so close to a championship only to lose. But there was some good news for LeBron in early 2007 to counter the disappointment of the Finals. Savannah gave birth to the couple's second son, Bryce Maximus James, on June 14, 2007. LeBron was the father of a new baby again, a role he loved.

That summer was a hectic one for LeBron, with a two-year-old and a newborn at home. In addition to family life and working on his game, LeBron made public appearances, such as cohosting the Excellence in Sports Performance Yearly (ESPY) awards with comedian Jimmy Kimmel. LeBron was nominated for three awards: Best Male Athlete, Best Record-Breaking Performance (for his historic double-overtime playoff game against the Pistons), and Best NBA Player. LeBron also

Funnyman: LeBron laughs while delivering the opening monologue on *Saturday Night Live* in 2007. His performance earned good reviews.

showed off his acting skills and sense of humor when he hosted the season opener of longtime late-night comedy show *Saturday Night Live* on September 29, 2007.

A New Season

In the fall, LeBron was all about basketball again. But he was not himself at the beginning of the 2007–2008 season. In the first game, for the first time ever in the NBA, LeBron failed to score a single point! Two games later, when the Cavaliers faced the New York Knicks, LeBron came alive, scoring 45 points, 7 rebounds, and 7 assists. King James, as he had come to be called, seemed back to normal.

LeBron continued to give back to his community, and he held a memorable charity event for the 2007 Thanksgiving holiday. During previous Thanksgivings, LeBron had given away turkeys to needy families, but he decided to do something different in 2007. He treated 800 families, many of whom were homeless, to a Thanksgiving feast with all the trimmings at Quicken Loans Arena where the Cavs play. After the meal, everyone watched the new movie *Alvin and the Chipmunks*, which had not yet been released in theaters. LeBron also handed out gift cards for groceries and other things, and everyone got to tour the Cavs' locker room.

LeBron has a personal chef named Brandon Taylor. Taylor prepares food for LeBron and his friends and family, and Taylor typically cooks for more than twenty people each day. According to the chef, LeBron's favorite food is lasagna.

Family: LeBron's mother Gloria *(left)*, partner Savannah *(center)*, and son LeBron Jr. look on during a Cavaliers' game early in the 2007–2008 season.

"It's great to see the smiles on kids' faces," LeBron said after the Thanksgiving event. "That's the most important thing to me. It really means a lot to them and it's special for me."

After his slow start to the season, LeBron went on a tear, racking up triple-doubles and helping his team rack up wins. In a seven-game stretch from November 14 to 27, LeBron scored more than 30 points in each game and averaged 9.3 rebounds and 10 assists. The Cavaliers were looking unstoppable until a game near the end of November against the Pistons. LeBron sprained his left index finger when the ball was batted from his hands. He was removed from the game and didn't return. Cavaliers players and fans were worried.

"[LeBron] makes a lot of our guys better, and he makes me look like I know how to coach a little bit," Coach Brown said. "I have faith and confidence in our guys, but in the big picture we can't get it done without him."

Unfortunately for Cleveland, Brown was right. The Cavaliers lost all five games that LeBron was forced to sit out due to his injury. When

he finally made it back onto the court, the team started winning games again. The 2007–2008 season was looking less rosy than the Cavaliers had hoped, though. They did not have a winning record heading into January, and there was talk that they might not make it back to the playoffs. Maybe LeBron heard the whispers, because he helped turn the season around for his team, leading them from a 14–17 record to 25–20 over the next 14 games. He had another 50–point game during this span, the fourth of his career, but he also suffered another injury. LeBron sprained his ankle but played through the pain.

Benched: After LeBron (*above*) sprained his finger against the Pistons, he had to sit on the bench and watch his team lose five straight games.

After LeBron's ankle injury, the Cavaliers realized that he was too valuable to lose. They decided to add more powerful players to protect LeBron and take some of the pressure of carrying the team away from him. The Cavs traded for four new players: Joe Smith and Ben Wallace came from the Chicago Bulls, and Wally Szczerbiak and Delonte West from the Seattle SuperSonics (now the Oklahoma City Thunder). Cleveland had some rough nights adjusting to the new players, but they won more games than they lost and ended the season 45–37. The Cavs were headed back to the playoffs.

LeBron had a regular season of ups and downs, but it was a successful year by most standards. He made his fourth All-Star appearance and was named MVP of the game, leading his Eastern Conference team to victory. He had seven triple-doubles during the season, making 17 for his career, a new team record. In a game against the Boston Celtics, LeBron became the youngest NBA player ever to score 10,000 career points. And with an average of 30 points per game, he also took home the NBA scoring title. But LeBron knew that his 2007–2008 season would be judged on how well he and his team did in the playoffs.

10,000 and counting: LeBron *(center)* goes up for a layup against the Boston Celtics on February 27, 2008. He became the youngest player to score 10,000 points in the NBA.

April 8, 2008

James flashes MVP pedigree

From the Pages of USA TODAY

He's only in his fifth year, but the on-court exploits of Cleveland Cavaliers forward LeBron James have already earned him a hip version of his nickname, "King James." Spelled phonetically, James [fans] often refer to him as "The Ka-a-a-a-ng."

Only the true greats receive this kind of treatment, and James stands worthy. "The numbers he's putting up this season," says Cavaliers coach Mike Brown, "compare to one or two guys in the history of the game."

James is averaging 30.2 points, 7.9 rebounds, 7.3 assists, 1.9 steals and 1.1 blocks per game this season. Granted, those numbers don't immediately strike you, not when compared to the 1961–62 accomplishments of Philadelphia Warriors center Wilt Chamberlain and Cincinnati Royals guard Oscar Robertson. Chamberlain averaged 50.4 points and 25.7 rebounds per game that year, while Robertson averaged a triple-double (30.8 points, 12.5 rebounds and 11.4 assists per game).

But what puts James in singular company is his consistency across the stat line. According to the Elias Sports Bureau, since the league began tracking steals and blocks in the 1973–74 season, no player has averaged at least 30 points, 7.9 boards, 7 assists, 1.8 steals and 1.0 blocks per game in a season with a minimum of 70 games played.

Even if you take away the steals requirement, no other in that span equaled James' numbers this year. His ability to score, see the floor and block shots makes him one of the NBA's all-time rare talents.

Take away the blocked shots, and the list remains exceedingly short: James and Michael Jordan, who averaged 32.5 points, 8.0 rebounds, 8.0 assists and 2.9 steals in the 1988–89 season (he fell short only in blocked shots, at 0.8 per game).

James has been able to post these numbers despite a lineup jumbled because of injuries. Two of the Cavaliers' top players—center Zydrunas Ilgauskas and guard Daniel Gibson—have missed a combined 32 games this year.

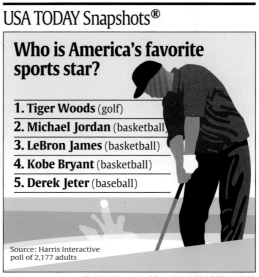

USA TODAY Snapshots®

Who is America's favorite sports star?

1. Tiger Woods (golf)
2. Michael Jordan (basketball)
3. LeBron James (basketball)
4. Kobe Bryant (basketball)
5. Derek Jeter (baseball)

Source: Harris Interactive poll of 2,177 adults

By Matt Young and Sam Ward, USA TODAY, 2009

"It's been very difficult to go out every night and not know who's going to be in the lineup," James says. "It's not like we've had guys sitting out for a couple of games; we've had guys out for weeks."

Because James is one of the NBA's most high-profile stars, it seems odd that this unique season seems to be getting short shrift nationally. Perhaps because he's so good, people have begun to take him for granted.

Or maybe it's because his team—which made it to the Finals last season—has struggled this year (42–35), so James isn't a serious candidate for league most valuable player honors. And lower back spasms have hampered him a bit recently.

"Voting is part team, part numbers, and part how valuable you are to your team," ESPN analyst Jon Barry says. "The Cavaliers' record eliminates him right off the bat. But LeBron is having an Oscar Robertson-type season."

—Chris Colston

Another Championship Run

LeBron was happy about the awards he'd received and the records he'd set in 2007–2008, but the biggest prize was the NBA championship. The Cavaliers' first playoff opponents that year were the Washington Wizards.

Rally: LeBron scored 42 combined points in Games Three and Four of the 2007–2008 Eastern Conference Semifinals. The Cavs won both games.

The series was marked by trash talk and hard play by both teams. In Game Two, Wizards player Brendan Haywood shoved LeBron so hard that Haywood was ejected from the game. Cleveland overcame the drama and put the ups and downs of the regular season behind them by beating Washington in six games. With the Wizards out of the way, the Cavaliers moved on to face the Boston Celtics in the Eastern Conference Semifinals.

After the first two games of the series, it looked as if it might be a Celtics sweep. LeBron was getting shut down by Boston's

The Boston Celtics have won the NBA championship 17 times, more than any other team. The Los Angeles Lakers are second with 16 NBA championships.

defense and was missing open shots from the floor. Once the series moved to Cleveland for Game Three, however, LeBron and his teammates came alive. Fired up by the home crowd and feeling the pressure of being down two games, LeBron went on a scoring rampage and led his team to two victories in a row.

With the series tied at two games each, Game Five moved back to Boston. The Celtics won on their home court and took the series lead, 3–2. Game Six was in Cleveland, and the home team won again, 74–69. The series was now tied at 3–3 and headed back to Boston. The Celtics won a nail-biting Game Seven, 97–92, and took the series. Boston went on to defeat the Los Angeles Lakers in the NBA Finals.

Once again, the Cavaliers were sent home without winning the NBA championship. Cleveland, a city that had not won a major professional sports title since 1964 (the NFL's Cleveland Browns), would have to wait at least one more season to see if the Cavs could make it happen. LeBron was open about his feelings. "I am at the point in my career now, if I don't win an NBA championship, it's a failure," he admitted.

LeBron was the reigning NBA scoring leader, but he was the first to admit he was not perfect. He knew he would have to play even better to reach his dream of an NBA championship. "I'm not the greatest of shooters," he said after being knocked out of the playoffs in 2008. "I'm not the greatest defender. I'm not the greatest rebounder or the greatest scorer. [But] I got everything in my game that can add up to a complete basketball player."

World beaters: LeBron *(right)* scores two points against Spain during the Olympic Games in 2008.

The Redeem Team

LeBron took his frustration to a new continent that summer, traveling to Beijing, China, for the 2008 Summer Olympic Games. Team USA's loss at the 2004 Olympic Games was still fresh in the memories of many Americans. The 2008 team wanted to bring home the gold medal and erase those bad memories.

The 12 players who made up Team USA, including stars such as LeBron, Kobe Bryant, Dwight Howard, and Dwyane Wade, were some of the best in the game and called themselves the Redeem Team. Their wins over China, Angola, Greece, Spain, and Germany by an average of 32.2 points in the qualifying round were impressive. In the quarterfinals, Team USA beat Australia, and in the semifinals, they took down Argentina. On August 24, 2008, the Redeem Team beat Spain for the second time in the tournament, 118–107, to win the gold medal.

While overjoyed for his team, LeBron was already preparing for the upcoming NBA season and trying to improve his game. His teammates knew that LeBron worked hard on his basketball skills. "A lot of times, people see him step on the court and do the things he does and go 'Wow,'" said teammate Zydrunas Ilgauskas. "What they don't see is 99% of the work that goes in before the game, the hours and hours in film session he spends, the hours in the weight room, the hours he spends shooting before practice, the hours shooting after practice."

Fresh from his team's victory in the Olympics, LeBron was eager to resume Cleveland's quest for the NBA championship that the team and the fans wanted so badly. But even before the season started, people were talking about what would happen in two years' time when

Winners: LeBron *(center)* and his Team USA teammates hold up their gold medals in 2008.

Betrayal: LeBron proudly displays his New York Yankees hat at a Cleveland Indians baseball game in 2007. Some people thought LeBron should have shown more loyalty to the hometown team.

LeBron's contract with the Cavaliers would expire. Many worried he would go to New Jersey or New York or another big-market team. "These [Cavaliers] fans have welcomed me with open arms and welcomed my family," LeBron said. "Me being a businessman has to understand that, in 2010, if the situation is right, then I will be here. But you can't throw your eggs in one basket. That's just being smart. At the end of the day, I'm happy here. We'll see what happens in 2010."

Quotes from LeBron about his future and the business of basketball made Cavaliers fans nervous. Many did not want to think about the possibility of their star player on a different team. Cleveland fans already had reason to doubt LeBron's loyalty thanks to an incident the year before. During the 2007 baseball playoffs, LeBron went to a Cleveland Indians Division Series game against the New York Yankees wearing a Yankees hat. LeBron said that while he loved his home state and its fans, he also rooted for the Yankees in baseball, the Dallas Cowboys in football, and the Chicago Bulls in basketball (unless they were playing the Cavaliers, of course). LeBron laughed off the controversy, but Cavaliers fans didn't think that the possibility of losing their state's biggest sports star was a laughing matter.

Focused: LeBron (*center*) seemed more determined than ever in 2008–2009.

More Than a Game

LeBron was not looking forward or backward as he prepared for the 2008–2009 NBA season. Instead, he was focusing on the present. While many did not see how it was possible for LeBron to be a better basketball player, he believed he could improve. He hit the gym and the court harder than ever before. "He wants to be first. He hates to lose no matter what we're doing. He wants to win at everything," teammate Daniel Gibson said.

LeBron was usually the first at

practice in the morning and the last to leave. He was also typically the first player to arrive at the airport for away games. He wanted to set a good example of not running late and being respectful to the team.

LeBron was now a veteran with five seasons under his belt and the Cavaliers unofficial leader. The rookies looked to him for advice even though some of them were just a year or two younger than 23-year-old LeBron. "I lose sight of the fact of how young I am," LeBron said. "When rookies come on your team and they're 20 years old, I call them youngsters, and I'm only 23 years old." Gibson recalls being helped by LeBron early in his career: "[LeBron's] a genuine person. From the moment I got here, he just took me in as his little brother."

Year of the Cavalier

LeBron improved his game and reached new statistical records during the 2008–2009 season. He set career highs in shots blocked (93), free-throw shooting percentage (78 percent), and free throws made (594). In fact, LeBron led his team in all five major basketball statistics: total points, rebounds, assists, steals, and blocks. This marked only the fourth time in NBA history that one player led his team in all five categories. He was named the NBA's Player of the Month in 2008–2009 a record four times.

With LeBron at the top of his game, it was no surprise that the Cavaliers had their best season so far with a record of 66 wins and only 16

USA TODAY Snapshots®

LeBron leads in steals

In only his sixth season in the league, LeBron James continues to stake his place in the Cleveland Cavaliers record books in steals. Here are the Cavs all-time leaders in steals.

LeBron James, 2003-current	**747**
Mark Price, 1986-95	**734**
Foots Walker, 1974-80	**722**
Craig Ehlo, 1986-93	**661**
Terrell Brandon, 1991-97	**621**

Source: Cleveland Cavaliers

By Matthew Cooper and Alejandro Gonzalez, USA TODAY, 2008

losses. This was the best record in the NBA and gave them a great position in the playoffs. Finally, they seemed to be on their way to winning it all.

Cleveland's first matchup was against the Detroit Pistons. The Cavaliers swept the series with LeBron averaging 32 points, 11.3 rebounds, and 7.5 assists per game. Near the end of Game Four, Cleveland fans at the arena chanted "M-V-P!, M-V-P!" for LeBron. They wanted him to be named NBA MVP for the first time.

On Monday, May 4, those fans got their wish when LeBron was announced as the NBA's 2008–2009 MVP. Sportswriters vote to give this honor to one player each year. LeBron received 109 of the possible 121 votes. Los Angeles Lakers star Kobe Bryant came in second, and the Miami Heat's Dwyane Wade was third. LeBron was the first Cavaliers player to ever receive the honor.

To make the prize even more special, LeBron accepted the MVP award in front of a hometown crowd at the SVSM gym where he'd played so many high school games. LeBron thanked his family and his Cavaliers

The best: LeBron holds the 2008–2009 NBA MVP award. Overhead are the banners celebrating the three state championships SVSM won while LeBron attended the high school.

teammates. "You never think something like this is going to happen to you, growing up in Akron," he said. "I never thought it would happen this fast." LeBron was the youngest player to receive the NBA MVP award since Moses Malone in 1979.

Cavaliers fans were very happy for their hometown sports hero. "You think of everything going on in Cleveland," said former Cavaliers head coach Mike Fratello after the announcement of LeBron's MVP award. "The city hasn't won a [major sports] title since 1964. Then you consider the economy, the unemployment rate, home foreclosures, the corruption of the political system downtown, all those things. LeBron is this bright light coming along, a local athlete, and everybody wants to attach to that. They want to root for him. They say, 'He's one of ours.'"

LeBron did not have time to rest after receiving his award. It was time to face the Atlanta Hawks in the 2008–2009 Eastern Conference Semifinals. As they had in the first round of the playoffs against the Pistons, the Cavaliers swept the series against the Hawks, winning every game. Cleveland looked unstoppable. Then they faced the Orlando Magic in the Eastern Conference Finals.

Before each game, LeBron rubs powder on his hands and then throws some into the air. The powder helps LeBron grip the basketball.

The Magic took the first game in the series and appeared ready to win the second until LeBron hit a miraculous three-pointer with no time left on the clock to win it, 96–95. The series was tied, 1–1. The Cavaliers lost the next two games in Orlando and trailed in the series, three games to one. The Cavs returned home to win Game Five. Trailing in the series three games to two, Cleveland had to win Games Six and Seven to advance to the NBA Finals.

May 27, 2009

LeBron still needs co-star

From the Pages of
<u>USA TODAY</u>

ORLANDO—The Orlando Magic lead the NBA's Eastern Conference finals 3–1, and it would be over if not for LeBron James' dramatic three-pointer at the buzzer to win Game 2 for the Cleveland Cavaliers.

James continues to get little help from his supporting cast. While Michael Jordan had his Scottie Pippen during his Chicago Bulls glory years, James is still searching for a sidekick to take pressure off him.

Guard Mo Williams, acquired in the offseason, was supposed to be that player. During the regular season he was, averaging 17.8 points and making the All-Star Game. But he has struggled mightily in this series, including 5–for-15 from the field Tuesday as the Cavaliers lost 116–114 in overtime.

While Williams continues to struggle from the field, the Magic offense continues to sizzle.

Orlando shot 50% from the field against a team that held opponents to 43% shooting during the regular season. The Magic had a playoff-franchise-record 17 three-pointers.

After allowing 78.1 points a game in the first two rounds—both series sweeps—the Cavaliers are allowing 104.3 to the Magic.

Now Orlando is one win from going to the NBA Finals for the first time since 1995.

"You can almost taste it," said guard Rafer Alston, who scored 26 points, including going 6–for-12 from three-point range. "We understand we have to win one more, and it won't be easy. But we are starting to taste it."

Magic coach Stan Van Gundy wouldn't have any of that talk, however. "The way I look at it, we're up two at the end of the third quarter. That's all I look at," he said. "This thing is a long, long, long way from over."

Van Gundy emphasized that in the postgame locker room.

"After the game was over, you would've thought we lost," said Orlando forward Rashard Lewis, who scored 10 of his 17 points in the fourth quarter. "He told us we

Tough shot: The Magic played tough defense against LeBron *(second from right).*

can't be relaxed. Anything can happen. We have to go into Cleveland hoping to close these guys out."

Van Gundy and the Magic certainly won't be able to relax for the rest of the play-offs, because Howard picked up his sixth technical foul of the postseason in Game 6. One more and he will be suspended for one game.

"Every time he gets a foul called against him or there is contact in paint, I cringe," Alston said. "It seems like he's going to say something that warrants a tech. I hope he understands this is a crucial time for him and for us as a team. If will lose him for a game, that's going to hurt us."

After getting his fifth technical in Game 3, Howard had said he might have to put duct tape over his mouth.

"I was just playing with emotion," he said of his sixth technical. "You score a big bucket, you let your emotions take over. It was a tough play. (Anderson Varejao) grabbed me around my neck, and I made the shot. I hope (the NBA will) look at it. But whatever happens, I have confidence in my teammates."

—Chris Colston

Magic men: LeBron *(right)* scored 37 points against the Orlando Magic in Game Five of the Eastern Conference Finals. LeBron's Cavs won the game, 112–102.

LeBron put up 25 points in the crucial Game Six. He played well, but it was just not enough. The Magic won the game and the series. Disappointed to be headed home once again without the championship, LeBron left the court without shaking hands with Orlando's players. Many people were surprised and took this as poor sportsmanship by LeBron. "It's not being a poor sport or anything like that," LeBron said later. "If somebody beats you up, you're not going to congratulate them. . . . I'm a competitor. That's what I do. It doesn't make sense for me to go over and shake somebody's hand."

A Ring for the King?

LeBron did charity work during the summer of 2009 and promoted his book *Shooting Stars*. Cowritten by LeBron and professional writer Buzz Bissinger, *Shooting Stars* details LeBron's days in Akron playing for the team that shared a name with the book's title. A documentary film

Movie night: LeBron arrives at a showing of *More Than a Game* in August 2009.

about LeBron's high school years titled *More Than a Game* was also released around this time. But despite the many distractions, LeBron's mind was on basketball and the NBA season ahead.

While gearing up for the 2009–2010 basketball season, LeBron and his teammates received some exciting news. Cleveland had traded for four-time NBA champion Shaquille O'Neal from the Phoenix Suns. LeBron was thrilled to have another superstar on the team. Shaq would force opposing defenses to concentrate on him near the basket, potentially leaving LeBron with more space on the court. The big center had averaged 17.8 points and 8.4 rebounds per game the year before with Phoenix.

Shaq made it known that he wanted to help LeBron and his team win a championship and finally get a ring. "Hopefully, I, we, can get this city, get this team over the hump," he said. At 37 years of age, Shaq was seen as the big brother of the team. He was also wise enough to know this team really belonged to LeBron.

IN FOCUS

Shaquille O'Neal

Shaquille O'Neal was born March 6, 1972. At 7 feet 1 inch (2.16 meters) and 325 pounds (147.4 kilograms), Shaq is one of the biggest men to ever play in the NBA. He won the NBA championship three years in a row (2000, 2001, and 2002) with the Los Angeles Lakers. Shaq won a fourth championship with the Miami Heat in 2006.

The Big Aristotle: Shaquille O'Neal *(left)* is one of the NBA's most successful players. His addition to the Cavs was a big deal for LeBron and the team.

Shaq was there to help. Former Cleveland assistant coach John Kuester said: "First of all, LeBron will make Shaq better. I just know that certain times, players need a change of scenery. This is a great change of scenery for Shaq, because he really seems committed to what they want to get done. I can see it being a good match."

While LeBron and the rest of the Cavs were excited about the new member of the team, two other people were also thrilled. LeBron's young sons, 5–year-old LeBron Jr. and 2–year-old Bryce, were big fans of Shaq. And Shaq loved hanging out with the boys before and after practices, even teaching little LeBron a special handshake.

Right away, LeBron and Shaq bonded on and off the court. "Me and Shaq are a great 1–2 punch, and we know we're very dominant. At the same time, you got to have three other guys on the court and 10 other guys on the bench that's making sure everything is going right also." LeBron and Shaq premiered together on an NBA court in October 2009. It appeared that the Cavaliers were going to have another amazing season.

Father figure: LeBron's sons LeBron Jr. *(front)* and Bryce *(center)* spent a lot of time around the Cavs. The boys were excited when Shaq joined the team.

LeBron was voted to the All-Star Game for the sixth time in his short career, and his Eastern Conference team won the game, 141–139. Later in the season, in a March 15 win over the Chicago Bulls, LeBron became the youngest player to score 15,000 regular-season points in

NBA history. LeBron was known for his incredible ability to make baskets and help his team rack up points, but he was just as important to the Cavs on defense. In addition to closely guarding his opponent on every possession, the star forward had become a master at what is known as the chase-down block. As the other team raced down the court on a fast break for a potentially easy basket, LeBron would use his remarkable speed and jumping ability to catch up to the player with the ball and block his shot from behind. "You've got to be conscious of where he's at all the time," Boston Celtics coach Doc Rivers said of LeBron. "I think he's more dangerous without the ball at times than with the ball."

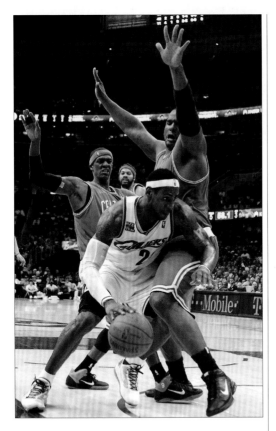

Knocked out: The Celtics defense was all over LeBron *(front)* during the 2009–2010 Eastern Conference Finals.

With LeBron and Shaq leading the way, the Cavaliers had the NBA's best regular-season record for the second year in a row, tallying 61 wins and 21 losses in 2009–2010. Also for the second year in a row, LeBron was named NBA MVP. He was glad for the honor, but LeBron was focused on basketball's ultimate prize: the NBA championship.

First up for the Cavaliers in the playoffs were the Chicago Bulls. The Cavaliers had home court advantage, and they won the series, 4–1. Coming off the high of beating the Bulls, the Cavaliers faced a tough Boston Celtics team in the Eastern Conference Semifinals. It appeared as though the Cavs were on their way to a series victory after winning two of the first three games. But then the Cavs collapsed, and the Celtics won the next three games to take the series.

Game Five against Boston was especially tough for LeBron as he made only three of 14 shots and scored just 15 points. The game was nicknamed "The Collapse" by sportswriters as the Cavaliers lost, 120–88. Cleveland fans even booed their hometown star. LeBron made no excuses for the inconsistency of his play, saying: "If I'm a fan from Cleveland and watching the game, I would have booed, too." Once again, people were talking about LeBron's inability to help his team win the big game. The criticism was unfair based on LeBron's many great performances in important games in the past, but Cleveland fans everywhere were disappointed by the dismal end to the season. It was a bitter and familiar theme.

"Please Don't Leave 23": A young fan signs a petition on a car asking LeBron to stay in Cleveland.

Free Agent

After the 2009–2010 NBA season ended, people were buzzing about what would happen with LeBron. His contract with Cleveland had expired, and the city and the team were nervous that he might leave. LeBron had taken the team to the NBA Finals and won two MVP awards. He provided a huge financial benefit to the Cavaliers and to Cleveland by increasing merchandise and ticket sales. LeBron knew that Cleveland was counting on him, but he also realized that professional basketball is a business.

Despite years of frustration and the heartbreaking loss to the Celtics in the 2009–2010 playoffs, Cleveland fans wanted LeBron to stay with the team. By NBA rules, the Cavaliers were able to offer him more money than any other team. Most people expected LeBron to accept the Cavaliers' offer to stay with the team that drafted him.

On July 1, 2010, at 12:01 A.M., LeBron became a free agent. Rumors ran wild about where he would end up. LeBron was a hot ticket, and many teams in the NBA were trying to get him, including the Knicks, the Nets, the Heat, the Bulls, the Dallas Mavericks, the Los Angeles Clippers, and of course the Cavaliers. Seven days later, LeBron announced on television that he planned to leave Cleveland and join the Miami Heat.

Fallout

After LeBron announced his intention to sign with Miami, many Cavaliers fans and employees turned on him. Some fans burned his jersey. Just after "The Decision" aired on ESPN, Cavaliers owner Dan Gilbert released an open letter to the fans about LeBron and the team's future that was both bitter and biting. He was later fined $100,000 by NBA commissioner David Stern.

Unhappy owner: Cavaliers owner Dan Gilbert *(above)* was upset that LeBron left Cleveland for Miami. Gilbert considered LeBron a traitor.

July 9, 2010

Cleveland frustrated again

From the Pages of
USA TODAY

Cleveland's sports history took another hit Thursday when LeBron James announced he was leaving the Cleveland Cavaliers for the Miami Heat. Cleveland fans remember these events all too well:

The Drive: The Cleveland Browns were less than six minutes from a 20–13 victory in the AFC Championship Game and the organization's first trip to the Super Bowl, in January 1987. The Denver Broncos muffed the kickoff, and quarterback John Elway took over at the Broncos' 2-yard line.

Six passes, three rushes and a couple of Elway scrambles later, Denver had tied the score with 37 seconds left. The Broncos won in overtime with a field goal.

The Fumble: A year after The Drive, the Broncos had a seven-point lead with four minutes to play in the AFC Championship Game vs. Cleveland in January 1988.

The Browns moved the ball to the Broncos' 8-yard line with 1:12 left in the game. Running back Earnest Byner got the handoff, took off for the end zone but was stripped by Jeremiah Castille and fumbled at the 2-yard line.

Denver recovered, gave the Browns an intentional safety and won 38–33.

Cleveland is one of four NFL teams never to have reached the Super Bowl.

The Shot: In the fifth and deciding game of the first round of the 1989 NBA playoffs, the Cleveland Cavaliers had a 100–99 lead against the Chicago Bulls with three seconds left.

Michael Jordan got the inbounds pass and shot over defender Craig Ehlo. The basket counted at the buzzer, leaving the Cleveland crowd stunned, the first of many such game-winning shots in Jordan's playoff career.

The Move: Art Modell, who owned the Browns for 35 years, had promised he would never move the team from Cleveland. But after the 1995 season, he began secret discussions with the state of Maryland about placing a team in Baltimore, which had lost the Colts to Indianapolis in 1984.

When the move was announced, fan reaction was overwhelmingly negative. Cleveland sued for breach of the stadium lease. The Browns franchise was ultimately deactivated for three years. With the 1999 season, the NFL gave the city an expansion team, which took the Browns name and colors.

The Collapse: The Cavaliers were the top seed in the Eastern Conference this past season after 61 wins. Led by James' 31.8 points a game, Cleveland cruised through the first round vs. the Bulls.

In the second round, the Cavs took a 1–0 series lead on the Boston Celtics. Boston won Game 2 on Cleveland's court, but the Cavaliers buried the Celtics 124–95 in Game 3 in Boston. The series seemed all but over.

Inexplicably, the Cavs came out flat the next three games and couldn't score more than 88 points in three consecutive losses. James, at times, looked uninterested. The conference's top team was knocked out, leaving James still looking for his first championship and Cavaliers fans wondering if they had seen the last of him in a home uniform.

The Decision: Or, as Cleveland fans will see it, The Failed Decision.

Controversial Cav: Lebron lets out a yell on the court.

ESPN's one-hour special, The Decision, sent Cleveland fans into a frenzy before James revealed where he would next play. He not only angered them by abandoning his hometown team but also humiliated them in what they saw as an over-the-top, prime-time debacle.

—Nicole Auerbach

IN FOCUS

Number 23

LeBron had worn the same jersey number (23) as his hero Michael Jordan since high school. But after the 2009–2010 season, LeBron announced that he would change his jersey number to 6. He felt that Jordan was such a great player that no one in the NBA should ever wear the number 23 again in Jordan's honor.

While many people agreed with Gilbert's passionate letter, others thought the owner had gone too far and was taking the issue too personally. Gilbert's sports memorabilia company, Fathead, lowered the price of its LeBron James wall graphics from $99.99 to $17.41. The year 1741 is when the famous traitor Benedict Arnold was born.

Despite the controversy surrounding LeBron's move, he was sure he had made the right decision for himself and his family. He regretted the bad feelings he'd left behind in Cleveland, but he was proud of what he'd been able to accomplish with his celebrity status. Proceeds from "The Decision" helped thousands of underprivileged kids. "I would do it again,"

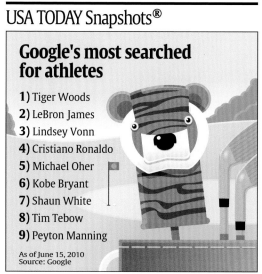

USA TODAY Snapshots®

Google's most searched for athletes

1) Tiger Woods
2) LeBron James
3) Lindsey Vonn
4) Cristiano Ronaldo
5) Michael Oher
6) Kobe Bryant
7) Shaun White
8) Tim Tebow
9) Peyton Manning

As of June 15, 2010
Source: Google

By George Artsitas and Paul Trap, USA TODAY, 2010

LeBron said. "I won't play this game forever. But the things we're doing in the communities, things that we're doing in the gymnasiums, in the computer labs, they will last. When I'm done playing basketball, I can still go back to those same parks and see what we were able to accomplish that day. . . . That's important to me."

On July 9, 2010, LeBron officially became a member of the Heat when Cleveland and Miami completed the deal that sent LeBron to Florida. The Cavaliers received three future draft picks and other considerations from the agreement. The Heat quickly hosted a rally at American Airlines Arena for about 13,000 fans who were thrilled to have LeBron and Chris Bosh, who had also just agreed to sign with Miami, join the team. LeBron's new contract was for six years and a staggering $109.8 million.

Party time: LeBron *(right)*, Chris Bosh *(center)* and Dwyane Wade *(left)* greet Heat fans at American Airlines Arena on July 9, 2010.

New digs: LeBron's home *(above)* in Miami is a waterfront mansion on Biscayne Bay.

Move to Miami

The summer of 2010 was a busy one for LeBron. "To move to a new state is not fun—trying to figure out your family situation, figure out where you'll be living, figuring out new routes to your work. That's not fun," LeBron told *USA Today*. The Heat's new star and his family eventually moved into a $9 million mansion overlooking Biscayne Bay in Miami's Coconut Grove neighborhood.

LeBron quickly began working with his new teammates to create chemistry on the court. LeBron bonded with Bosh and Wade as well as former Cavaliers center Zydrunas Ilgauskas. Z, as Ilgauskas is called, is a great friend to LeBron and joined the Heat for the 2010–2011 season. Having Z on the team helped ease LeBron's transition to Miami. The players had mutual admiration for each other. "I wanted him to succeed, because from Day 1 I saw something special in him, and we could have something special," Z said. "I knew players like that do not

Chris Bosh

Chris Bosh played seven seasons with the Toronto Raptors before joining the Miami Heat for the 2010–2011 season. The 6-foot-10-inch center has been named to the NBA All-Star Game each year since 2005–2006. He has averaged 19.8 points per game in nine NBA seasons.

walk into your locker room every year. You'd be lucky to play your career with one of those guys."

The two players were friends on and off the court, and their families were happy to be reunited in Miami. LeBron's sons, 6–year-old LeBron Jr. and 3–year-old Bryce, were friends with Z's two adopted sons, 6–year-old Deividas and 5–year-old Povilas. This friendship would serve the families well as they settled down in Miami and got ready for the much anticipated 2010–2011 season.

Big Z: At 7 feet 3 inches (2.22 meters) and 260 pounds (117.9 kilograms), Zydrunas Ilguaskas *(above)* is usually the tallest player on the floor.

Shouldering the burden: When he joined the Heat, LeBron was under a lot of pressure to help make the team winners.

Turning Up the Heat

■ ■ ■ ■

Before he even stepped foot on the court with the Miami Heat for the 2010–2011 NBA season, LeBron was one of the most talked about sports figures in the country. But since "The Decision" had aired in July, the talk was not always positive. LeBron had gone from being a well-loved and respected player with a growing list of NBA records to a sort of basketball villain in the

New guy: LeBron *(center)* worked with his new Heat teammates and coaches before the start of the 2010–2011 season.

minds of many. He knew that the best way to improve his standing with basketball fans was to win games on the court.

LeBron and his new teammates worked on plays and got to know one another before the start of the new season. But injuries plagued the Heat, and LeBron, Wade, and Bosh only managed three minutes of play together in preseason games. They would need to come together quickly as a team once the regular season started.

In addition to the normal preparations a team has to make for an NBA season, Miami faced a tremendous amount of extra pressure and high expectations. LeBron, Wade, and Bosh were considered three of the best players in the NBA, and LeBron had specifically come to Miami because he thought it was his best chance to win. Anything short of winning the NBA Finals would be a disappointment. "No team since I've been affiliated with the NBA has had more pressure on them to win—not just win, but win multiple championships," said former NBA star Charles Barkley. "If you look at it from a realistic standpoint, if they only win one championship for the next five years, it's got to be viewed upon as a failure."

First Season

Ready or not and with the eyes of the basketball world on the Heat, LeBron and his new team took on the Celtics in the 2010–2011 season opener in Boston. The matchup drew the biggest ratings ever for a regular-season NBA game on cable television. Unfortunately for the Heat, their performance did not live up to the hype. Wade, Bosh, and LeBron, who were nicknamed the Threetles by the media, had obviously not yet found their rhythm as a team. The Threetles is a reference to the famous rock band the Beatles, who generated hysteria wherever they went. LeBron said he preferred to be called the Heatles.

No matter which nickname stuck to the Heat stars, they had some growing to do as a team. LeBron, Wade, and Bosh were each used to being the stars of their teams and played best with the ball in their hands. Finding ways to share the ball and play with teamwork was going to take some effort.

The Heatles: LeBron *(left)*, Bosh *(center)*, and Wade *(right)* take the court for the first game of the 2010–2011 season.

The Heat scored just nine points in the first quarter against Boston. Even though LeBron racked up 31 points by the end of the game, the Heat lost to the Celtics, 88–80. It was a disappointing start to the new season, and the Boston crowd chanted "overrated!" to the Heat as they left the court. "It's a feel-out process," LeBron said of getting used to playing with his new teammates. "We have so many options. It's something I'm not accustomed to, having that many threats on the court."

Next up for the Heat were the 76ers in Philadelphia, a city known for having vocal

Good start: LeBron *(above)* played well in his first game with the Heat, even though the team lost.

fans at sporting events. LeBron was booed and called names. But despite the rough treatment, the Heat were coming together on the court and starting to get a feel for their strengths and weaknesses. LeBron and his teammates played more aggressively than they had against Boston, and the effort paid off with a 97–87 win over the 76ers.

The Heat lost about as many games as they won through the first couple of months of the season. But LeBron had some personal success mixed in with the team's highs and lows. On November 2, he had a game-high 12 assists in a win over the Minnesota Timberwolves. This was the most assists in a game in team history by a forward. The Heat beat Minnesota, 129–97. One week later, LeBron had his 29th career triple-double and his first with the Heat, tallying 20 points, 14 assists, and 11 rebounds in a 116–114 loss to the Utah Jazz.

Facing the Cavaliers

The Heat were still playing unevenly in early December when they faced the Cavaliers in Cleveland for one of the most anticipated games of the 2010–2011 season. Cavs' fans were still bitter about the way LeBron had left the team and were hungry for a victory over the Heat. The December 2 game was a sellout with extra cameras added to catch all the action and extra security to handle more than 20,000 rowdy fans.

LeBron slept little the night before the game as he worried about what would happen. "I'm ready for whatever response I'm going to get," he said. "It's going to be very emotional. I give a lot of thanks to that city, to those fans for giving me the opportunity to not only showcase my talent, but to grow from a boy to a young man during my seven years. So it's going to be very emotionally draining."

The good feelings for Cleveland that LeBron expressed were not returned to him that night. There were anti-LeBron rallies held throughout the city before the game. For security reasons, fans had to go through metal detectors before entering the arena. Once inside, drinks were sold in plastic cups to prevent bottles and cans from being thrown onto the court. LeBron endured the angry shouts and signs of Cavaliers fans, but there was little violence. One person was arrested, and four people were ejected from the game.

"When it comes down to it, if people didn't react to him, it would show they didn't care," fan and LeBron documentary filmmaker Kirsten Brownrigg told *USA Today*. "It really is a testament to how much he meant to the city, how important he was and how much of an influence

Hometown villain: Cavaliers fans made sure that LeBron *(above)* didn't feel welcome when he returned to Quicken Loans Arena in 2010, the first time since switching teams.

he was. . . . If they hadn't loved him so much, they wouldn't hate him so much."

With the Heat struggling to find their rhythm early in the season and the Cavaliers playing better than expected, many Cleveland fans thought they had a chance to beat LeBron and Miami. But the Heat players were on fire that night in Cleveland, and LeBron was their brightest flame. He started out slowly but then came alive as the game went on, scoring a season-high 38 points. The once-rowdy crowd settled down by halftime and was quiet by the time the game ended in a Heat blowout over the Cavaliers, 118–90. In addition to his impressive point total, LeBron committed no turnovers and played tough defense. The crowd's anger had fueled LeBron's desire to win, and the game was a sign of things to come. The Heat won their next 10 games in a row, including another win against the Cavaliers in Miami, while Cleveland lost their next 10 games.

December 3, 2010

In hostile environment, James gives Heat jolt

From the Pages of USA TODAY Who would have figured the only thing the Miami Heat needed to kick-start their season was a visit to Cleveland to face the Cavaliers?

Instead of fearing this game, facing and conquering his former team is what forward LeBron James needed to perhaps get Miami's season turned around.

James made his first shot and didn't stop making shots until late in the third quarter. By then, he had a season-high 38 points, with eight assists and five rebounds, and the Heat were on their way to a commanding 118–90 victory Thursday.

"I'm very exhausted," James said of his emotional return. "I didn't get much sleep last night. I didn't get much sleep today. I'm glad we played well as a team."

James didn't even need to play in the fourth quarter.

Nearly a week after a players-only meeting following a loss to the Dallas Mavericks, and a confab between James and Heat coach Erik Spoelstra, the Heat (12–8) have won three in a row.

Spoelstra spoke to the team of what was important: coming together. "We are a family, and we'll take care of our two brothers," Spoelstra said of James and former Cavaliers center Zydrunas Ilgauskas. "And you do that collectively by making ourselves feel normal and doing this together.

"The second thing is this is an extreme environment here tonight. There's no way around that. We want to stay in the moment as much as possible."

They were in the moment. Guard Dwyane Wade had 22 points, nine rebounds and nine assists, forward James Jones had 18 points off the bench (five three-pointers) and forward Chris Bosh had 15 points.

But James was the centerpiece, leading up to and during one of the most hyped games of the season. The game started with boos for James and cheers for Cavaliers owner Dan Gilbert. But the night ended belonging to James. He said he didn't take anything the fans said personally.

"I have to maintain my focus no matter what's said or done during that game," he said.

James dominated, especially in the third quarter, scoring 24 points on 10–for–12 shooting. At one point the Heat had an 88–50 lead, their largest of the season, and the final ended up as Cleveland's biggest loss.

Also on James' final stat sheet: zero turnovers. He entered leading the league in turnovers; it was his first game without one.

Undaunted: LeBron (*above*) scored 38 points in his return to Cleveland, almost 12 points more than his average for the 2010–2011 season.

It was also a night for Ilgauskas who spent the first 12 seasons of his NBA career with the Cavaliers and is that team's all-time leader in games played. He followed James to Miami in the offseason. His reception was much warmer than that for James, who was booed and jeered.

The Heat visit the Toronto Raptors on Feb. 16 and hope to do the same for Bosh, who left Toronto for Miami.

"We know we haven't played up to par against plus-.500 teams," James said. "We're going to try to keep this momentum going."

—Jeff Zillgitt

IN F**O**CUS

Dwyane Wade

Dwyane Wade has what LeBron has been seeking for years: an NBA championship. Wade and his Heat teammates beat the Dallas Mavericks in the 2005–2006 NBA Finals. Wade was named MVP of the NBA Finals that year.

Next up for the Heat was a matchup with the New York Knicks, a game many thought could also turn ugly. After all, LeBron had chosen Miami over New York, and the Knicks and their fans did not like to lose. But the game was peaceful and the Heat won, thanks in part to LeBron's second triple-double of the season with 32 points, 11 rebounds, and 10 assists.

The Heat seemed to be warming up in the season's second half. They were 34–14 on February 3, 2011, as they headed into an important game against the Orlando Magic, Miami's intrastate rival and a tough team. Orlando fell to the Heat, 104–100. LeBron scored a season-high 51 points, with 11 rebounds and eight assists.

Once again, LeBron was chosen to start for

USA TODAY Snapshots®

Most popular NBA jerseys since start of 2010-11 season

1. **LeBron James,** Miami Heat
2. **Kobe Bryant,** Los Angeles Lakers
3. **Rajon Rondo,** Boston Celtics
4. **Amar'e Stoudemire,** New York Knicks
5. **Derrick Rose,** Chicago Bulls

Source: The Associated Press

By Matt Young and Sam Ward, USA TODAY, 2011

the Eastern Conference in the All-Star Game. He was joined on the team by Heat teammates Wade and Bosh. LeBron had a triple-double, but his effort didn't result in a win for the East. The All-Star Game loss seemed to follow the Heat after the break, as they went on a five-game losing streak. But the team rallied to win 15 of their final 18 games, improving their record enough to take them back to the playoffs.

Turning Up the Heat

LeBron finished the 2010–2011 regular season ranked second in the NBA in scoring with 26.7 points per game, while Wade was fourth with 25.5 points per game. Together, they scored 4,052 points for the season, a Heat record for a pair of teammates. But LeBron and Wade both knew that their season would be judged by how the team performed in the playoffs.

First up for the Heat were the 76ers. Philadelphia was overmatched, and Miami took the series, four games to one. The Heat next faced the Boston Celtics in the Eastern Conference Semifinals. Boston was a team full of tough, veteran players. The matchup was one

Surrounded: LeBron *(second from left)* draws a crowd as he drives to the basket against Boston.

Taking flight: LeBron *(center)* soars to the hoop during Game Two of the 2010–2011 Eastern Conference Finals.

everyone was excited to watch. Even Miami fans, known for arriving late to games and leaving early, seemed more energized than usual. The Heat won the first game on their home court, 99–90.

The Heat won Game Two of the series by an even bigger margin, 102–91. The biggest problem for the Celtics was which of the Heat players to focus on shutting down. LeBron, Wade, and Bosh formed a nearly unstoppable force on the court. "Tonight was only our seventh playoff game together. We just try to continue to get better . . . just try to be great every night if we can," LeBron said. Heat coach Erik Spoelstra said it was LeBron's attitude that set the tone for the night's win. "LeBron was physically, mentally, and emotionally tough for us," Coach Spoelstra said.

The series moved to Boston for Game Three, where the Celtics won, 97–81. They were cheered on by an enthusiastic hometown crowd. The fourth game was a Heat victory thanks in large part to LeBron's 35 points and 14 rebounds. It was the first time Miami had won in Boston in five years. A 10-point win, 97–87, over the Celtics in Game Five meant the Heat would move on to face the Chicago Bulls in the Eastern Conference Finals.

Things looked good for Miami early in Game One against Chicago, as

LeBron started the game with a block, a rebound, an assist, a steal, and a dunk in the first 41 seconds. From there the game fell apart for the Heat, however, resulting in a 103–82 Bulls victory. The Heat bounced back for Game Two. Although he was battling a cold, LeBron played as if he were feeling fine and the Heat won, 85–75. Bosh stepped up his effort in Game Three to score 34 points and help lead the Heat to another win. With an overtime win in Game Four, the Heat were anxious to finish off the Bulls in Game Five. LeBron, with help from his teammates, made it happen for his new team. Miami won the game, 83–80. The Heat were headed to the NBA Finals!

The Heat were fired up and ready to face the Dallas Mavericks for a chance to be NBA champions. Game One was fiercely contested, but the Heat were clearly the dominant team. Miami excelled at defense, rebounding, and three-point shooting. LeBron was quiet for the first half of the game but came alive in the third quarter, posting 24 points,

Posterized: LeBron *(left)* throws down a vicious dunk while Dirk Nowitzki *(center)* and Tyson Chandler *(right)* of the Mavericks look on.

nine rebounds, and five assists by the end of the night. It was LeBron's first NBA Finals win as the Heat took down the Mavericks, 92–84.

The Mavericks took Game Two by just two points, 95–93. The Heat rallied to win another close game, 88–86, in Game Three to put them up two games to one. LeBron was well on his way to capturing the championship ring he had been dreaming about since childhood. But the Mavericks fought hard in Game Four and the Heat lost, 86–83. The series was tied, 2–2.

LeBron played poorly in Game Four, scoring only eight points, but he didn't make excuses. "I was hard on myself all night," LeBron said. "If it was the Super Bowl, I'd be kicking myself. The great thing about this is, it's a series. No matter if you have a bad game, you can always make an imprint on the next game." LeBron knew he needed to step up for Game Five.

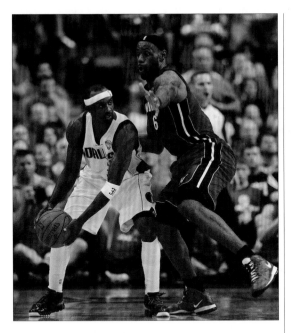

Shut down: LeBron *(right)* stays close to Mavericks guard Jason Terry. Miami held Dallas to just 86 points in Game Four, but the Heat could only muster 83 points and lost the game.

Game Five, held on June 9, 2011, was critical for LeBron and Miami. But despite his 17 points, 10 rebounds, and 10 assists, the Heat lost, 112–103. LeBron racked up a triple-double in the game, but some people thought he should have scored more points. "I had a bad game in a lot of people's eyes," he said. "I understand that." Fans and reporters were again saying that LeBron buckled in the high-pressure environment of the NBA Finals. "I think the game of basketball can be pressure," LeBron said after Game Five. "It doesn't matter if it's the Finals or the Conference Finals or first round. Playoff basketball is all about pressure, how you can handle it."

Miami would need to win the next two games to take the series. LeBron led his team with 21 points, but the Mavericks won Game Six in Miami, 105–95, to become NBA champions. LeBron and his team-mates were crushed. But LeBron showed good sportsmanship and gave credit to the Mavericks, saying, "They did a great job every time I drove, brought another defender in front of me. They're a very under-rated defensive team. . . . It hurts of course, but I'm not going to hang my head low. I know how much work as a team we put into it, how much I put into it. . . ." LeBron's 17.8 points, 6.8 assists, and 7.1 re-bounds per game during the NBA Finals were good statistics, but some people expected more from one of the NBA's best players.

Many NBA fans were happy with the outcome, especially those who disagreed with LeBron's decision to leave the Cavaliers. While Dallas celebrated winning the NBA championship, so did some peo-ple in Cleveland. Still angry with his former star, Cavaliers owner Dan Gilbert sent a message through Twitter congratulating the Mavericks. Ohio governor John Kasich called the Mavericks and their fans "honor-ary Ohioans."

Family and the Future

After the disappointing end to the 2010–2011 NBA season, LeBron turned his focus away from the basketball court. He continued to do charity work for underprivileged children and in September was hon-ored with the Champion of Youth Award by the Boys & Girls Clubs of America. LeBron mentioned his own childhood in his acceptance speech for the award. "I was one of those underprivileged kids where people thought we were a statistic and didn't have a way out and would fall into traps of life and our surroundings," he said. "For these kids to

Kid friendly: LeBron speaks to children at an event for the LeBron James Family Foundation in 2011.

kids to have a way out, that's amazing and I'm happy to be a part of it."

LeBron was anxious for another shot at the NBA Finals, but the 2011–2012 season was in jeopardy due to arguments between owners and players about how to distribute profits. Negotiations went on for months and some games were canceled. A deal was finally reached and the NBA announced that the first games of the season would be played on December 25, 2011. But basketball wasn't the only thing on LeBron's mind at this time. On January 1, 2012, LeBron and longtime girlfriend Samantha Brinson became engaged to be married.

LeBron seemed to be on a mission from the beginning of the 2011–2012 season. He scored 37 points and led the Heat to victory over the defending NBA champion Dallas Mavericks, 105–94, on December 25. He kept up the hot pace and finished the season with a 27.1 points-per-game average, third-best in the NBA. Even better, the Heat had the second-best record in the Eastern Conference and were headed back to the playoffs.

LeBron and the Heat rolled past the competition to reach the NBA Finals for the second year in a row. They would face the Oklahoma City Thunder. This time, LeBron was determined to bring home the

Finally: LeBron holds the championship trophy after his team beat the Thunder in the 2012 Finals.

big prize. In the decisive Game Five, he put up a triple-double with 26 points, 11 rebounds, and 13 assists. The Heat won the game, 121–106, and took the series. The title that LeBron had dreamed about for so long was finally his. "I'm an NBA champion," he said after the game. LeBron was named Finals MVP for his amazing efforts.

Miami reached the Finals for the third straight year in 2013. They faced a new team in the San Antonio Spurs, but the result was the same. LeBron and the Heat were NBA champions again. And for the second year in a row, LeBron was named MVP of the Finals.

LeBron James will be a force on the basketball court for a long time to come. He has the skills, dedication, and passion to become one of the best players in the history of the game. His legacy may one day even rival that of his favorite player, Michael Jordan. But for now, LeBron is happy to be known as an NBA champion.

CAREER STATISTICS

REGULAR SEASON

Year	Team	GP	GS	MPG	FG%	3P%	FT%	RPG	APG	SPG	BPG	PPG
2003–04	Cleveland	79	79	39.5	.417	.290	.754	5.5	5.9	1.6	0.7	20.9
2004–05	Cleveland	80	80	42.4	.472	.351	.750	7.4	7.2	2.2	0.6	27.2
2005–06	Cleveland	79	79	42.5	.480	.335	.738	7.0	6.6	1.6	0.8	31.4
2006–07	Cleveland	78	78	40.9	.476	.319	.698	6.7	6.0	1.6	0.7	27.3
2007–08	Cleveland	75	74	40.4	.484	.315	.712	7.9	7.2	1.8	1.1	30.0
2008–09	Cleveland	81	81	37.7	.489	.344	.780	7.6	7.2	1.7	1.1	28.4
2009–10	Cleveland	76	76	39.0	.503	.333	.767	7.3	8.6	1.6	1.0	29.7
2010–11	Miami	79	79	38.8	.510	.330	.759	7.5	7.0	1.6	0.6	26.7
2011–12	Miami	62	62	37.5	.531	.362	.771	7.9	6.2	1.9	0.8	27.1
2012–13	Miami	76	76	37.8	.565	.406	.753	8.0	7.2	1.7	0.9	26.8
Career		765	764	39.6	.492	.338	.748	7.3	6.9	1.7	0.9	27.6
All-Star		9	9	30.7	.517	.397	.724	6.6	6.0	1.3	0.2	25.1

PLAYOFFS

Year	Team	GP	GS	MPG	FG%	3P%	FT%	RPG	APG	SPG	BPG	PPG
2006	Cleveland	13	13	46.5	.476	.333	.737	8.1	5.8	1.4	0.7	30.8
2007	Cleveland	20	20	44.7	.416	.280	.755	8.1	8.0	1.7	0.5	25.1
2008	Cleveland	13	13	42.5	.411	.257	.731	7.8	7.6	1.8	1.3	28.2
2009	Cleveland	14	14	41.4	.510	.333	.749	9.1	7.3	1.6	0.9	35.3
2010	Cleveland	11	11	41.8	.502	.400	.733	9.3	7.6	1.7	1.8	29.1
2011	Miami	21	21	43.9	.466	.353	.763	8.4	5.9	1.7	1.2	23.7
2012	Miami	23	23	42.7	.500	.259	.739	9.7	5.6	1.8	0.6	30.3
2013	Miami	23	23	41.7	.491	.375	.777	8.4	6.6	1.8	0.8	25.9
Career		138	138	43.1	.472	.322	.749	8.6	6.7	1.7	0.9	28.1

Key: GP: games played; GS: games started; MPG: minutes per game; FG%: field-goal percentage; 3P%: three-point percentage; FT%: free-throw percentage; RPG: rebounds per game; APG: assists per game; SPG: steals per game; BPG: blocks per game; PPG: points per game

GLOSSARY

controversy: a dispute or argument between two sides with different views

debut: the first public appearance of someone or something

draft: the selection of people for a team or organization

eligibility: qualifications for play

endorse: to give support to someone or something

forfeit: to lose the right to something by breaking certain rules or not making requirements

lockout: temporary closing of a business or refusal by an employer to allow employees to come to work until they accept the employer's terms

rookie: a person new to a job or team

turnover: loss of control of the ball to the opposing team

versatility: able to do many things well

SOURCE NOTES

5 Associated Press, "LeBron James Extends Charity Efforts," *ESPN.com*, March 2, 2011, http://sports.espn.go.com/nba/truehoop/miamiheat /news/story?id=6175574 (March 14, 2012).

6 Jeff Zillgitt, "Judgment Day Is Here," *USA Today*, July 8, 2010.

6 Ibid.

7 ESPN, "LeBron James' Decision: The Transcript," *ESPN.com*, July 8, 2010, http://espn.go.com/blog/truehoop/post/_/id/17853/lebron-james-decision-the-transcript (March 15, 2012).

7 Ibid.

7 Ibid.

9 Matt Christopher, *On the Court with . . . LeBron James* (New York: Little, Brown and Company, 2008), 5.

11 Sal Ruibal, "At 17, Hottest Hoopster: LeBron James Makes Money for Everyone but Himself, for Now," *USA Today*, December 11, 2002.

11 Sal Ruibal, "Life Is a Bowl of Cereal for Player of the Year," *USA Today*, May 8, 2002.

12 Christopher, *On the Court with . . . LeBron James*, 15.

13 Ray Glier, "Sky's Limit for USA's Top Prep Basketball Player," *USA Today*, November 20, 2001.

15 Carolyn White, "Ohio Sophomore Sets Tongues Wagging," *USA Today*, February 6, 2001.

17 Glier, "Sky's Limit for USA's Top Prep Basketball Player."

17 Christopher, *On the Court with . . . LeBron James*, 32.

19 Ruibal, "At 17, Hottest Hoopster: LeBron James Makes Money for Everyone but Himself, for Now."

19 Ibid.

24 Christopher, *On the Court with . . . LeBron James*, 50.

26 Roscoe Nance, "LeBron Just Plays It Cool," *USA Today*, June 24, 2003.

28–29 Ibid.

29 Nance, "LeBron Just Plays It Cool."

34 Ryan Jones, *King James: Believe the Hype—the LeBron James Story* (New York: St. Martin's Press, 2005), 216.

35 David DuPree, "LeBron or D-Wade; Who Is the Best in the NBA?" *USA Today*, October 31, 2006.

36 Jones, *King James: Believe the Hype—the LeBron James Story*, 217–218.

39 DuPree, "LeBron or D-Wade; Who Is the Best in the NBA?"

46–47 Christopher, *On the Court with . . . LeBron James*, 78.

48 David DuPree, "Living up to All the Hype," *USA Today*, June 4, 2007.

49–50 Ibid.

51 Associated Press, "LeBron, Cavaliers Outlast Pistons in Game 5," June 1, 2007, http://www.nba.com/games/20070531/CLEDET/recap.html (April 10, 2012).

55 Julie Kent, "LeBron James Also Proves That He's the King of Charity," *Cleveland Leader*, November 19, 2007.

56 Roscoe Nance, "Cavaliers Hoping to Weather Loss of LeBron," *USA Today*, November 29, 2007, http://www.usatoday.com/sports /basketball/nba/2007–11–29–east-notes_N.htm (March 16, 2012).

61 Jeff Zillgitt, "The King Without a Crown," *USA Today*, October 28, 2008.

61 Ibid.

63 Zillgitt, "Judgment Day Is Here."

64 Ibid.

66 Ibid.

67 Ibid.

67 Ibid.

69 Chris Colston, "The Chosen One: LeBron Is MVP," *USA Today*, May 5, 2009.

69 Ibid.

72 William Rhoden, "A Handshake Is Not Too Much to Ask, Even from a King," *New York Times*, June 2, 2009.

73 Jeff Zilgitt, "LeBron's New Right-Hand Man," *USA Today*, October 27, 2009.

74 Ibid.

75 Ibid.

76 Jonathan Abrams, "On Defense, James Is Closer Than He Appears," *New York Times*, May 5, 2010, http://www.nytimes.com/2010/05/06 /sports/basketball/06cavs.html (April 10, 2012).

77 Jeff Zillgitt, "Cleveland to LeBron: Fare Well," *USA Today*, May 13, 2010.

82–83 Associated Press, "LeBron James Extends Charity Efforts."

84 Jeff Zillgitt, "In a Sunshine State of Mind," *USA Today*, October 19, 2010.

84–85 Ibid.

87 Michael McCarthy, "The New Team We Love to Hate," *USA Today*, October 22, 2010.

89 Jeff Zillgitt, "In Opener, Celtics Hold Off Heat," *USA Today*, October 27, 2010.

90 Jeff Zillgitt, "City Ready to Vent at the King," *USA Today*, December 2, 2010.

90–91 Ibid.

96 Jeff Zillgitt, "James, Wade on a Roll," *USA Today*, May 4, 2011.

96 Ibid.

98 Mike Lopresti, "A Non-Factor in Game 4," *USA Today*, June 9, 2011.

98 Dean Schabner, "LeBron James Choking? Numbers Say Yes, Miami Heat Star Says No," *ABC News*, June 12, 2011, http://abcnews .go.com/Sports/lebron-james-choking-numbers-miami-heat-star /story?id=13823358#.T4RTq9UlOZQ (April 10, 2012).

99 Ibid.

99 J. Michael Falgoust, "Ohio Rejoices in James' Failure to Win Title," *USA Today*, June 13, 2011.

99–100 Associated Press, "Boys & Girls Clubs Honor LeBron James," *ESPN .com*, September 21, 2011, http://espn.go.com/nba/truehoop /miamiheat/story/_/id/7000557/lebron-james-honored-boys-girls- clubs-america-champion-youth (March 16, 2012).

101 "LeBron Leaves No Doubt With First Crown," *ESPN.com*, June 22, 2012, http://sports.espn.go.com/nba/dailydime (6/22/12).

SELECTED BIBLIOGRAPHY

Christopher, Matt. *On the Court with . . . LeBron James*. New York: Little Brown and Company, 2008.

Jones, Ryan. *King James: Believe the Hype—the LeBron James Story*. New York: St. Martin's Press, 2005.

Morgan, David Lee, Jr. *LeBron James: The Rise of a Star*. Cleveland: Gray & Company, Publishers, 2003.

FURTHER READING AND WEBSITES

Books

Freedman, Lew. *LeBron James: A Biography*. Westport, CT: Greenwood Press, 2008.

Kennedy, Mike, and Mark Stewart. *Swish: The Quest for Basketball's Perfect Shot*. Minneapolis: Millbrook Press, 2009.

Pluto, Terry. *LeBron James: The Making of an MVP*. Cleveland: Gray & Company, Publishers, 2009.

Websites

Lebronjames.com—LeBron James' Official Website
http://www.lebronjames.com
LeBron's site includes information on LeBron both on and off the field, with photos, insider info, news, and more.

NBA.com—the Official Website of the National Basketball Association
http://www.nba.com
The NBA's official site includes scores, news, statistics, video features, and other information for basketball fans.

NBA.com/heat—the Official Website of the Miami Heat
http://www.nba.com/heat
Follow the Miami Heat on its official site, which features photos, videos, news, scores, and much more.

INDEX

PHOTO ACKNOWLEDGMENTS

The images in this book are used with the permission of: © Mike Ehrmann/Getty Images, pp. 1, 86; © Robert Hanashiro/USA TODAY, pp. 3, 81; © Larry Busacca/Getty Images, pp. 4, 6, 7; © Benkrut/Dreamstime.com, p. 8; © Craig Jones/Getty Images, p.10; © AF Archive/Alamy, pp. 11, 14; AP Photo/Tony Dejak, pp. 13, 23, 28, 36, 53, 91; © Aaron Josefczyk/Reuters/CORBIS, p. 15; Bob Falcetti/Icon SMI/Newscom, p. 16; © Tom Pidgeon/Getty Images, p. 18; Icon SMI/Newscom, p. 19; © Eliot J. Schechter/ USA TODAY, pp. 20, 30, 44, 58, 70, 80, 92; © Eileen Blass/USA TODAY, pp. 21, 24; AP Photo/Haraz Ghanbari, p. 25; © Robert Deutsch/USA TODAY, p. 26; © Ron Kuntz/ Reuters/CORBIS, pp. 27, 32; AP Photo/Stuart Ramson, p. 33; © H. Darr Beiser/USA TODAY, p. 34; © Streeter Lecka/Getty Images, p. 37; AP Photo/Mark J. Terrill, p. 38; © Gary Miller/FilmMagic/Getty Images, p. 39; AP Photo/Mark Duncan, pp. 40, 43, 55; Aaron Josefczyk/Reuters/Newscom, p. 41; John Gress/Reuters/Newscom, p. 42; © Joe Giza/Reuters/CORBIS, p. 46; Ed Suba Jr./Akron Beacon Journal/KRT/Newscom, p. 47; © Chris McGrath/Getty Images, p. 49; Andre Smith/Reuters/Newscom, p. 50; © Ronald Martinez/Getty Images, p. 52; © Dana Edelson/NBC Universal/Photofest, p. 54; Kirthmon F. Dozier/Detroit Free Press/MCT/Newscom, p. 56; AP Photo/Elise Amendola, p. 57; © Jim Rogash/Getty Images, p. 60; ZUMA Press/Newscom, pp. 62, 78; © Filippo Monteforte/AFP/Getty Images, p. 63; AP Photo/Amy Sancetta, pp. 64, 68, 73; © Jeff Haynes/Getty Images, p. 66; AP Photo/David Richard, p. 71; © Gregory Shamus/Getty Images, pp. 72, 74, 76, 79, 93, 96; © Jason Merritt/Getty Images, p. 75; © Marc Serota/Getty Images, p. 83; CelebrityHomePhotos/Newscom, p. 84; © Chris Graythen/Getty Images, p. 85; Joe Skipper/Reuters/Newscom, p. 87; © Charles Trainor Jr./Miami Herald/MCT/Newscom, p. 88; Matthew Healey/UPI/Newscom, p. 89; AP Photo/Charles Krupa, p. 95; © Don Emmert/Getty Images, p. 97; John G. Mabanglo/ EPA/Newscom, p. 98; AP Photo/Akron Beacon Journal, Ed Suba Jr., p. 100; © Don Emmert/AFP/Getty Images, p. 101.

Front cover: AP Photo/Wilfredo Lee.

Back cover: © Marc Serota/Getty Images.

Main body text set in USA TODAY Roman Regular 10.5/15.

ABOUT THE AUTHOR

Anne E. Hill has written more than 20 biographies and fiction books for children and young adults. One of her titles, *Denzel Washington*, was chosen one of The New York Public Library's Best Books for the Teen Age. She lives outside of Philadelphia, Pennsylvania, with her husband, daughter, and basketball-fan son, who urged her to write this book.